我的"一带一路"

成都市广播电视台"熊猫小记者"全球追访"一带一路"大型公益新闻接力行动

My "Belt and Road"
Global News Relaying on the Belt and Road by "Little Panda Reporters"
of Chengdu Radio & Television Station

成都市广播电视台 编

人民日报出版社

图书在版编目(CIP)数据

我的"一带一路":成都市广播电视台"熊猫小记者"全球追访"一带一路"大型公益新闻接力行动 / 成都市广播电视台编. —北京:人民日报出版社,2018.1

ISBN 978-7-5115-5325-6

Ⅰ.①我… Ⅱ.①成… Ⅲ.①"一带一路" –国际合作–青少年读物 Ⅳ.①F125 –49

中国版本图书馆 CIP 数据核字(2018)第 032831号

书　　名:	我的"一带一路":成都市广播电视台"熊猫小记者"全球追访"一带一路"大型公益新闻接力行动
作　　者:	成都市广播电视台
出 版 人:	董　伟
责任编辑:	刘晴晴
封面设计:	蓝狮文化/张群英
出版发行:	人民日报出版社
社　　址:	北京金台西路2号
邮政编码:	100733
发行热线:	(010)65369527　65369846　65369509　65369510
邮购热线:	(010)65369530　65363527
编辑热线:	(010)65363105
网　　址:	www. peopledailypress.com
经　　销:	新华书店
印　　刷:	成都市金雅迪彩色印刷有限公司
开　　本:	787mm×1092mm　　1/16
字　　数:	250 千字
印　　张:	21.5
印　　次:	2018 年10月第1 版　　2018 年10月第1 次印刷
书　　号:	ISBN 978-7-5115-5325-6
定　　价:	68.00 元

胸怀天下　　路在远方

　　2016年4月"世界读书日"期间，我被邀请到成都市几所小学与孩子们分享我新近出版的一些新书，分享阅读的快乐。课堂上，许多家长都急切地问到同一个问题：到底该给孩子阅读什么样的书，人生的第一本书应该读什么。经过认真思考，在几所学校里我都给出了同一个答案，那就是：爸爸妈妈们在孩子入学时首先要做的事，就是在家里给孩子挂上一幅世界地图、一幅中国地图。

　　从小把孩子置于世界的中央、置于国家的中央。第一，让孩子有了方位感；第二，孩子有了世界观；第三，孩子有了大胸怀。

　　我认为，这是一个孩子成长历程中最不可缺少的一环。

　　在我上小学一年级的时候，父亲给我的第一件礼物就是一幅巨大的中国地图，几乎把书房的一面墙壁铺满。还记得我童年最喜欢做的事除了阅读，就是趴在地图上，搜寻着滔滔黄河、滚滚长江；搜寻着长城内外、塞北江南；搜寻着李白的诗篇、徐霞客的足迹；搜寻着春秋战国的烽烟、五代十国的更替；搜寻着大明宫的辉煌、圆明园的日落……后来，父亲又给我挂上了一幅世界地图，从此视野更广阔、思维更宽广。这两幅地图带给我的不只是经纬度，不只是疆域国界，不只是风云雨雪，还有上下五千年的人类文明史。这两幅图促成了一个孩子世界观、方位感的养成，让一个孩子能够具体地感知我是谁，我在哪里，将来我想去哪里，哪里是滋养我的土地，哪里是我的诗和远方。

地图应该是一个孩子最早要读的东西。

由成都市广播电视台主办的"'熊猫小记者'全球追访'一带一路'大型公益新闻接力行动"按年度进行，每年开展两季行动，即夏季行动和冬季行动。目前2017年度所有行动已完美收官。此项活动属于国家广电总局"丝绸之路影视桥工程"全国重点项目。这是让孩子们走天下、看世界、长知识、促成长的一件大事。活动内容是由孩子们组成"熊猫小记者"出访团，分三批次经不同线路探访"一带一路"沿线国家和城市，了解这些国家和城市的历史文化和发展现状，以小记者的独特视角寻找和解读这些国家的文化与中国文化的交流与融合，探寻中国与这些国家如何通过"一带一路"的实施来实现交流发展、共建人类命运共同体。2017夏季行动为"走出去"，由国内的"熊猫小记者"组成张骞队、郑和队、马可·波罗队三支出访队，出访"一带一路"沿线十多个国家和地区，去感受"一带一路"构想的宏伟蓝图；2017冬季活动内容为"请进来"，邀请国外的"熊猫小记者"到中国成都来过新年，以国外小朋友的视角感受中国文化和天府文化，用他们的笔触宣传四川文化，讲述中国故事，传播华夏文明。

孩子们虽然年纪小，但却在遥远的路途中排除困难、认真刻苦、开动脑筋、独立自主，不仅出色地完成了任务，还锻炼了意志，增长了见识，获得了从身体到心灵的双重成长。

这是一项意义深远的活动，一项让孩子们走出校园、走上社会、走向世界的有着长远目标和现实意义的活动，一项让孩子们迅速成长、了解中国与世界的关系、学着承担起小主人公责任和使命的活动。

从来没有一个人是孤立的，每一个人都是广袤世界的一部分，孩子们也不例外。中国现代化进程日益加快，在将要实现中华民族伟大复兴的时代，年轻的一代更不能闭目塞听、孤芳自赏。中国的发展离不开世界，世界的未来需要中国参与。培养一代有学识、有教养、有担当、有使命的年轻人，正是祖国未来发展的需要，是民族复兴大业的需要。

从张骞出使西域到今天的"一带一路"倡议，丝绸之路上的驼铃一直传递着中国人民热情好客、开放包容的国家精神。"和平合作、开放包容、互学互鉴、互利共赢"的理念不仅促进了东西方经济的繁荣与发展，也同时促进了东西方文化的交流与发展，有效地消除民族区域隔阂，促进世界和平。孩子们就像这条丝路上的小小和平鸽，鸣响着欢乐的哨音，传达着快乐、自信、和谐和交融的讯息。

胸怀天下，路在远方。从小把国家和民族放在心里的孩子，会走得更稳；从小把世界和人类放在心里的孩子，会走得更远。

李牧雨
四川省文联国家一级作家
影视编剧
著名儿童文学作家

Minding the World, the Road is Long

During World Book Day in April, 2016, I was invited to several primary schools in Chengdu to share with children the joy of reading. I read some of my recent published books. In class, many parents were eager to know what books were proper for children to read and what to read at the very beginning. After careful thinking, my answer was as follows. Before children entering school, the thing for their parents to do is to put up a map of the world and a map of China at home.

In this way, since his or her childhood, a child has been positioned in the center of the world and in the center of the country. Firstly, the child can get a sense of orientation; secondly, the child can get a world view; thirdly, the child can get a broad mind.

I think this is the most indispensable part during a child's growth.

When I was in Grade One in primary school, my father's first gift to me was a huge map of China, which almost covered a wall of the study room in my home. In addition to reading books, my most favorable hobby during childhood was to read the map, enjoying searching for the surging Yellow River and Yangtze River, studying areas inside and outside the Great Wall, imagining beautiful Jiangnan (South China) in poems of Li Bai the famous poet, following footprint of Xu Xiake the great traveler, looking for battlefields of the Spring and Autumn Period and the Warring States Period, of Five Dynasties and Ten Kingdoms Period, admiring the glory of Daming Palace and Winter Palace... Later, my father hung a map of the world for me. Both my vision and my mind were broadened by reading these two maps. The maps demonstrated not only longitude and latitude of the globe, or the national boundary, but also the five-thousand-year history of China and the history of human civilization. The two maps shaped a child's world view and sense of position, let a child specifically perceive who am I, where I am, where to go in the future, where is my beloved motherland, where is my "poetry and the distance" (quotation of a song).

A map should be the thing for a child to read.

Each year, the " 'little panda reporters' global follow-up the Belt and Road news relaying" hosted by Chengdu Radio and Television Station is held in summer and winter. The summer and winter session in 2017 all turned out to be great success. This activity is part of the national key project of the

"Film and Television Bridge Project of the Silk Road" of the State Administration of Radio, Film and Television. It is a great event for children to travel around the world, see the world, gain knowledge, and develop. The "little panda reporters" in three groups visited countries and cities along the Road by different routes to understand these countries and historical culture and current situation of the development. From their unique perspective, they searched and interpreted culture exchange and the fusion between these national and China. They tried to explore how China and these countries work together to realize mutual development and build a community of shared future for mankind through the implementation of the Initiative. The summer session of the project in 2017 is "going out". Domestic "little panda reporters" visited the countries and cities along the Belt and Road in three batches, namely Zhang Qian Team, Zheng He Team and Marco Polo Team, all the way along more than ten countries and regions, to feel the grandeur of the Initiative. The winter session is "inviting in". Foreign "little panda reporters" were invited to Chengdu, China during the Spring Festival, to experience and promote the culture of China and Chengdu the Land of Abundance, to tell Chinese stories from their perspective and thus spread the Chinese civilization.

Though very young, being creative and independent, "little panda reporters" went through distant journey despite all difficulties. They not only successfully finished the task, but also gained knowledge, courage and strong will, both their bodies and minds were developed accordingly.

In a whole, this is a far-reaching project. This is a project with a long-term goal and practical significance. Children are encouraged to go out of the campus, into the society and towards the world. This is the very project that children needed for a rapid growth. Through these activities, children will learn to shoulder responsibility and learn more about the relationship between China and the world.

No one is an island, and everyone is part of the vast continent. Children are no exception. In the era of China's accelerating modernization and the realization of the great rejuvenation of the Chinese nation, the younger generation must not indulge in self-admiration and be out of touch of the reality. China cannot develop in isolation from the rest of the world, and the future of the world needs China's participation. It is the need of the future development of our country to train a generation of educated, civilized, responsible and mission-oriented young people.

From Zhang Qian's journey to the Western Region in the past to the Belt and Road initiative at present, the camel bell ringing on the Silk Road has always conveyed the Chinese people's hospitality and openness and inclusiveness. The concept of "peace and cooperation, openness and inclusiveness, mutual learning, mutual benefit and win-win" concept is not only to promote the prosperity of eastern and western economic development, but also to promote the communication and development of eastern and western cultures, effectively break down the barriers between the ethnic regions, promote world peace. The children, like little pigeons on the Silk Road, whistle joyfully, conveying happy, confident and harmonious messages.

Minding the world, the road is long. Children who have put the country and nation in their hearts from childhood will move forward more steadily. Children who have put the world and humanity in their hearts from childhood will go further.

Li Muyu

First level writer of the Federation of Literature (Sichuan Province)

Film Writer

Famous Children's Literature Writer

搭建中外文化交流与融合的桥梁

  我很高兴值此新春佳节之际，来到美丽的"天府之国"成都，与大家一同感受这里的节日气氛。在此，我谨代表国家新闻出版广电总局国际合作司对成都广播电视台举办的"'熊猫小记者'全球追访'一带一路'大型公益新闻接力行动"冬季活动——"外国家庭蓉城春节行"的顺利启动表示热烈的祝贺！

  去年8月，"熊猫小记者"夏季活动顺利举行，中国小记者们兵分三队，前往不同的"一带一路"沿线国家，开展了丰富多彩的采访交流活动，获得国内外各界的关注。今天，来自西班牙、德国、法国、匈牙利、波兰、俄罗斯、加拿大、澳大利亚、哈萨克斯坦、越南等10个"一带一路"沿线国家的小记者与我们相聚成都欢度春节，继续争当连接中国与世界的文明使者，搭建中外文化交流与融合的桥梁。

  春节是中华民族最重要的传统佳节，它蕴含着中华民族的智慧与结晶，凝聚着吉祥和喜庆、亲情和友情。中国有句古话："一年之计在于春。"春节是中国农历新年的第一天，而成都是"南丝绸之路"的第一站。时间与空间的起点交汇，这赋予了我们这次活动特别的意义。希望小记者们通过为期一周的活动，深入探寻中国春节的文化内涵，体会中国人在年岁之交对一年收获的喜悦以及对美好生活的向往和期待，并将这种人类共同追求的价值观传递给世界人民。

近年来，国家新闻出版广电总局围绕"一带一路"倡议，策划实施了"丝绸之路影视桥工程"，旨在发挥广播影视的桥梁纽带作用，加强与"一带一路"沿线国家民心相通，推动与世界各国不同民族的文化交流和合作。经过四年的努力，影视桥工程的引领作用和集合效应日益凸显，各省广播影视机构和民营企业积极参与，取得了显著成效。本次"熊猫小记者"活动，是"丝绸之路影视桥工程"重点项目之一。借此机会，我也代表国际合作司对成都广播电视台积极参与总局"丝绸之路影视桥工程"表示衷心感谢。今后，我们将一如既往关注成都、支持成都，与成都媒体同行一道，为讲好中国故事，传播中华文化，做出更大贡献。

最后，预祝"熊猫小记者"冬季活动圆满成功！祝在场各位新春快乐，阖家幸福！

（摘自国家新闻出版广电总局国际合作司副司长周继红于2018年2月13日在成都"熊猫小记者"冬季活动启动仪式上的讲话）

Forging the Bridge of Cultural Exchanges and Integration between China and Foreign Countries

It is a great pleasure for me to come to Chengdu, the beautiful city of abundance, to share the happiness here during this New Year. Here, on behalf of International Cooperation Department, the State Administration of Press, Publication, Radio, Film and Television, I would like to express my warm congratulations to the launching of "the Spring Festival of foreign families in Chengdu" ! I wish all go well with the winter session of the "little panda reporters" follow-up "the Belt and Road" global relaying hosted by Chengdu Radio and Television Station!

In August last year, summer session of the "little panda reporter" held successfully. Three teams of little Chinese reporters traveled to different countries along the Road, conducted a series of activities to enhance mutual exchange, and got the attention of all walks of life both at home and abroad. Today, little reporters from among Spain, Germany, France, Hungary, Poland, Russia, Canada, Australia, Kazakhstan, Vietnam and other 10 foreign countries along the Road, gather here to celebrate the Spring Festival in Chengdu with us. They will act as civilization messengers. They will help to forge the bridge between China and foreign countries, and contribute to our cultural exchanges and integration.

The Spring Festival is the most important traditional festival of the Chinese people. Full of lively atmosphere and friendly and family affection, Spring Festival shows the wisdom of the Chinese people. There is an old saying in China, "a year's plan is in the spring". The Spring Festival is the first day of the Chinese New Year, and Chengdu is the first stop of the south Silk Road. Time and space intersects here, which gives special meaning for this activity. Hopefully, through one week's activity, the cultural connotation of Chinese New Year will be probed. Little reporters may share the joy of harvest and yearning for a better life of Chinese people at the end of an old year and the beginning of a new one, and pass on this common pursuit of human value to the rest of the world.

In the spirit of the Belt and Road initiative, in recent years, the State Administration of Press, Publication, Radio, Film and Television implemented the "Film and Television Bridge Project of the Silk Road", which aims to play as a bridge to strengthen the connection of the hearts and minds of countries along the Road, to promote cultural exchange and cooperation with different nationalities. Through four years of efforts, the Bridge Project has played more and more important leading role. Provincial radio, film and television institutions and private enterprises also actively participated in this project and achieved remarkable results. This "little panda reporter" activity is one of the key projects of "Film and Television Bridge Project of the Silk Road". I, on behalf of International Cooperation Department, would like to take this opportunity to express my sincere gratitude to Chengdu Radio and Television Station for its active participation in the project. In the future, we will continue to pay close attention to Chengdu, support

Chengdu, and work with our peers in Chengdu to make greater contribution to tell the story of China and spread Chinese culture.

In a word, I wish the "little panda reporter" winter session a complete success! Wish you all a happy New Year and a happy family!

(An excerpt from Speech at the Launching Ceremony of the winter session of "little panda reporters" follow-up "the Belt and Road" global relaying, by Zhou Jihong, Deputy Director of the International Cooperation Department of the State Administration of Press, Publication, Radio, Film and Television, on February 13, 2018)

培养中波文化交流的小使者

我住在成都两年多了,感觉自由自在。 感谢我遇到的不同年龄的人。据我个人经验,了解外国人民、文化和传统最好的方式就是去当地访问,与当地人民交朋友,阅读与之相关的图书及文章,并观看相关电影。

我非常高兴,参加了成都市广播电视台组织的年度盛会——国家广电总局"丝绸之路影视桥工程"项目"'熊猫小记者'全球追访'一带一路'大型公益新闻接力行动"夏季和冬季活动。我非常感激,波兰被选为"熊猫小记者"的目的地之一。我相信,这次经历拉近了波兰与成都的距离,也希望有些小记者爱上波兰。这些年轻人未来将成为波中关系的使者。

波兰与四川的合作在不同维度发展, 其中之一是人文交流。自本学年起,波兰语在四川两所大学开课,许多波兰学生在成都学习汉语。成都本地幼儿园与波兰幼儿园进行了友好交流。我们领事馆与成都的中小学紧密合作。我们每年都会把波兰音乐家、艺术家、专家以及艺术、传统及美食带到成都。今年秋天,我们将再次在蓉举办"波兰文化节"活动。诚邀各位参加!

祝大家幸福美满,万事如意!

卡夏

波兰驻成都总领事

2018年5月18日

Cultivating Young Cultural Exchanges Ambassadors between China and Poland

I have been in Chengdu for more than two years. I felt very pleasant and carefree living in this city. Here I would like to express my gratitude to local people of all ages that I encountered. From my personal experience, the best way to learn about foreign people, culture and traditions is to visit the countries, to make friends to local people, to read a lot of books, articles and movies about them.

I'm very happy that in the summer and winter of 2017, I participated in the activities of " 'little panda reporters' of the Belt and Road global news relaying" which is part of the national key project of the "Film and Television Bridge Project of the Silk Road" of the State Administration of Press, Publication, Radio, Film and Television in 2017. I am very grateful that Poland was chosen as one of the destinations for "little panda reporters". I believe that this experience has brought Poland closer to Chengdu and hopefully some small reporters have fallen in love with Poland. These young people will become goodwill ambassadors between China and Poland.

The cooperation between Poland and Sichuan is developing at various levels, one of which is cultural exchange. Since the beginning of this semester, the polish language has been taught by two universities in

Sichuan. Many Polish students have studied Chinese in Chengdu. Local kindergartens in Chengdu have had exchanges with Polish kindergartens. Polish consulate works closely with the primary and secondary schools in Chengdu. We invite Polish musicians, artists, experts to Chengdu, along with Polish art, tradition and food to Chengdu every year. This fall, we will hold Polish cultural festival once more. We sincerely invite you to join us!

Wish you all a happy and prosperous life!

Kasha

Consul General of Poland Consulate General in Chengdu

May 18, 2018

目录

《我的「一带一路」》编者说

第一章 张骞队新闻行动

● 第二章 马可·波罗队新闻行动

第三章　郑和队新闻行动

Contents

Chapter Two: Marco Polo Team

Chapter Three: Zheng He Team

Chapter Four: Winter Session—"Trip to Chengdu in Chinese New Year"

Brief Introduction to Project of "Trip to Chengdu in Chinese New Year"

1. An's Belt and Road

2. "The Belt and Road" and Me

3. The Relationship between Hungary and China Have Reached a New Level

4. My Idea of "the Belt and Road"

5. Meeting in Chengdu in the Spring Festival of 2018

6. "The Belt and Road" in My Eyes

7. Why I Want to Go to China

8. A Brilliant Journey to China

9. A Special Trip to China

10. Cool Connection—CHINA RAILWAY Express

我的"一带一路"编者说

张骞队新闻行动

马可·波罗队新闻行动

郑和队新闻行动

冬季活动——"中国年·成都行"

中华民族历来是一个爱好和平的民族，也是一个重视与世界交流、共同发展的民族。远在汉代，张骞出使西域，打通了中原与西域、中亚、南亚，甚至欧洲的联系之路。在秦汉时期，中国南部沿海一些居民就通过船只与南亚国家有经贸往来。到了明代，郑和率领船队七下西洋，最远曾达东非、红海沿岸，中国与海上丝绸之路沿线国家的联系更加密切。元代时，西方的马可·波罗也来到中国，并把他在中国的见闻写在了《马可·波罗游记》中，让西方对当时的中国有了一定的了解。

而今，随着科技的发展、出行的方便，世界的联系越来越紧密。中国离不开世界，世界也离不开中国。为此，中国国家主席习近平在2013年提出了共建"丝绸之路经济带"和共同建设21世纪"海上丝绸之路"的倡议，即"一带一路"倡议。此倡议一提出，立即得到了沿线国家的热烈反响。因为"一带一路"虽然由中国倡议，却非中国独有。它既是中国推动构建人类命运共同体的实践平台，也是完善全球发展模式和全球治理、推进经济全球化健康发展的重要途径。

"一带一路"倡议的基石是民心相通。为了促进民心相通，作为南丝绸之路起点的成都行动了起来。2017年3月，我们精心策划了"'熊猫小记者'全球追访'一带一路'大型公益新闻接力行动"。此行动就是为了促进成都与"一带一路"沿线国家之间民心相通，增强成都的青少年与"一带一路"沿线国家青少年之间的沟通交流。活动坚持新闻性与公益性相统一，为此获得了中国国家广电总局的大力支持，入选2017—2018年度"丝绸之路影视桥工程"全国重点项目。

我们主办的"熊猫小记者"全球追访"一带一路"大型公益新闻接力行动按年度进行，每年开展两季行动，即夏季行动和冬季行动。夏季行动内容为"走出去"，是由国内的"熊猫小记者"分成张骞队、郑和队、马可·波罗队三支出访队，出访"一带一路"沿线十多个国家和地区，去感受"一带一路"构想的宏伟蓝图；冬季活动内容为"请进来"，邀请国外的"熊猫小记者"到中国过新年，以国外小朋友的视角去感受中国文化和天府文化，用他们的笔触讲述中国故事，传播华夏文明。

本书收录了2017年度夏季活动和冬季活动中外"熊猫小记者"的42篇文章。这些文章是孩子们在参与活动中的心理感受和心得体会。我们以孩子们的独特视角寻找和解读中西方文化的相互交流与融合，探寻中国与这些国家如何通过"一带一路"倡议的实施来实现相互交流发展，共建人类命运共同体。

为此我们编纂本书，就是希望更多的还没有参与此次公益活动的孩子能够通过阅读本书，去感受中西方文化的交流，领悟"一带一路"倡议所构建的美好未来，培养他们成为传递友谊的小使者。

截止本图书出版时，2018年"熊猫小记者"全球追访"一带一路"大型公益新闻接力行动（第二季）已完成了出访行动。2018年7月30日，40余名熊猫小记者分成张骞队、马可·波罗队、郑和队三支采访队伍，前往"一带一路"沿线国家波兰、捷克、匈牙利、德国、荷兰、比利时、老挝、柬埔寨、越南等进行采访和交流活动，现已安全返回成都。相较于去年，本次活动呈现出了许多新亮点：在参与范围上，首次将小记者选取范围拓展到了四川省和西南地区；在线路规划上，更加突出体验"一带一路"建设5年来的重大成果和与当地中小学生的交流互动，使小记者对"一带一路"印象更直接更真实；在宣传推广上，更加注重出访国所属媒体的宣传报道。我们除了邀请人民网、《四川日报》、四川广播电视台、三沙卫视和巴中广播电视台派出记者随团采访报道外，此次出访的"熊猫小记者"还特别注重与所在国媒体的交流，通过沿线国媒体的宣传报道，进一步增强了活动的国际影响力和传播力。

《我的"一带一路"》得以出版，一方面与国家广电总局国际合作司、人民日报出版社、四川省新闻出版广电局、成都市人民政府新闻办公室、成都市文化广电新闻出版局、成都市妇女联合会等单位的倾心指导分不开，同时成都彩虹集团、苏宁电器、成都电视发展有限公司和成都天府新区华阳街道办事处也给予了大力支持，在这里一并表示感谢！

因出版时间关系，本书仅仅收录了2018年夏季活动的部分照片，而40余名"熊猫小记者"的参观心得文章，将在《我的"一带一路"》后续出版物中呈现。如需了解更多内容，敬请关注成都市广播电视台"神鸟资讯"客户端相关报道。

2018年8月8日
成都市广播电视台

My "Belt and Road"
Editor's Word

The Chinese people are always peace-loving. We attach great importance to exchanges and common development with outside world. The history of Sino-foreign mutual exchanges may date as far back as to the Han Dynasty, when Zhang Qian traveled to the Western Region, opening up the links between the central plains of China and the Western Region, central Asia, South Asia and even Europe. During the Qin and Han dynasties, some sailors of China's southern coastal areas traded with south Asian countries. In the Ming Dynasty, Zheng He's seven voyages to the Western Seas reached as far as East Africa and the red sea coast. In the Yuan Dynasty, westerner Marco Polo also came to China and shared his experiences in China in his book *The Travels of Marco Polo*. His vivid portrait gave the westerner a certain understanding of China at that time.

Nowadays, with the development of modern science and technology, travelling becomes more and more convenient and the world is more and more closely connected. China's development cannot be isolated from the world's development and vice versa. Therefore, in 2013, Chinese President Xi Jinping proposed the initiative of the Belt and Road, that is to say, jointly building the Silk Road economic belt and the 21st century Maritime Silk Road. As soon as this Initiative was put forward, it received a warm response from countries along the roads. Although initiated by China, the Belt and Road initiative is not exclusive to China. It is a practice platform for promoting the building of a community of shared future for mankind, and it is an important approach to improve global development model and governance, promote the sound development of economic globalization as well.

The foundation of the Belt and Road initiative is people-to-people bond. Chengdu is the starting point of the southern Silk Road. So, in order to promote people-to-people ties, in March 2017, "little panda reporters" global follow-up Belt and Road news relaying was launched by Chengdu Radio and Television Station. We carefully planned this project, aimed at promoting mutual understanding between Chengdu and countries along the Road, and strengthening communication between Chengdu's youth and those of countries along the Road. This activity is a public welfare zeroing in on journalistic report. Therefore, it was selected as part of 2017–2018 national key project of the "Film and Television Bridge Project of the Silk Road" sponsored by the National Radio and Television Administration.

The "little panda reporters" global follow-up Belt and Road news relaying is carried out on an annual basis, with summer and winter sessions. Summer session is "going out". That is to say, domestic little panda reporters visited the countries and cities along the Belt and Road in three batches, namely Zhang Qian Team, Zheng He Team and Marco Polo Team, all the way along more than ten countries and regions, to feel the grandeur of the Initiative. The winter session is "inviting in". That is to say, foreign "little panda reporters" were invited to China during the Spring Festival, to experience and promote the culture of China and Chengdu, the Land of Abundance, to tell Chinese stories from their perspective and thus spread the Chinese civilization.

This book contains 42 articles by Chinese and foreign "little panda reporters" for the summer and winter sessions of 2017. These articles recorded the children's feelings and experiences in participating in this project. From children's unique perspective, we are to search for and interpret the mutual communication and integration of Chinese and western cultures, explore how China and these countries are going to implement the Initiative, towards realization of mutual communication and development, and towards building a community of shared future for mankind.

Hopefully that by reading this book, those who haven't participated in this activity may experience the culture communication, get the idea put forward by the Initiative of building a better future. May they be little messengers of Sino-foreign friendship!

By the time *My "Belt and Road"* was published, the "little panda reporters" follow-up "the Belt and Road" global relaying (the second session) has completed. On July 30, 2018, more than 40 little panda reporters started from Chengdu and visited countries along the Road, including Poland, Czech Republic, Hungary, Germany, Netherlands, Belgium, Laos, Cambodia and Vietnam, for interviews and exchange activities. They travelled in three teams, namely Zhang Qian team, Marco Polo team and Zheng He team. Now they have returned to Chengdu safe and sound. Compared with last year's activities, this session highlighted in many new aspects. For the first time, the little reporters involved expanded to Sichuan province and Southwest China. Major achievements of the Belt and Road initiative implementation in five years are demonstrated and communication and interaction with local primary and middle school students are in abundance. The little reporters gained direct and lively impression on "the Belt and Road". In this session, we zero in on the publicity and coverage of the local media. Not only reporters from news agencies including People.cn, *Sichuan Daily*, Sichuan Radio and TV Station, San Sha TV Station and Ba Zhong Radio and TV Station are invited to conduct interviews with the group, little panda reporters also communicate actively with local media. Through the publicity of local media, this project arouse international response.

Without the considerate guidance of the National Radio and Television Administration, People's Daily Press, Press, Publication, Radio, Film and Television of Sichuan Province, Information Office of the People's Government of Chengdu, Chengdu Culture, Radio and TV, Press and Publication Bureau and other news agencies, Chengdu Women's Federation, and of course, without sponsor from Chengdu Rainbow Group, Suning.com, Chengdu TV Development Co.,Ltd., and Huayang Subdistrict Office of Chengdu Tianfu New Area, the publication of My *"Belt and Road"* would not be possible. Let us take this chance to express our gratitude to you all!

Due to publication procedure, we only collect part of the photos during summer session of 2018 in this book. Articles of more than 40 little panda reporters' visiting experience will be presented in follow-up publication of My *"Belt and Road"*. For further information, please consult public accounts of CDTV News.

Chengdu Radio and TV Station
August 8, 2018

▲2017年8月4日，"熊猫小记者"全球追访"一带一路"大型公益新闻接力行动启动仪式上，"熊猫小记者"展示"伴手礼"

▲ 法国驻成都总领事馆副总领事卡维在"熊猫小记者"全球追访"一带一路"大型公益新闻接力行动启动仪式上致辞

▲"熊猫小记者"宣誓

▲ "熊猫小记者"宣誓

▲ 领队授旗

▲ 活动正式启动

▲马可·波罗队出发

▲郑和队从成都双流国际机场出发

第一章

张骞队
新闻行动

Chapter One

Zhang Qian Team

张骞 （前164—前114）

中国汉代杰出的外交家、旅行家、探险家，丝绸之路的开拓者。张骞先后两次出使西域，打通了汉朝通往西域的南北道路，即赫赫有名的丝绸之路。张骞被誉为 "丝绸之路的开拓者" "第一个睁开眼睛看世界的中国人" "东方的哥伦布"。他将中原文明传播至西域，又从西域诸国引进了汗血马、葡萄、苜蓿、石榴、胡麻等物种到中原，促进了东西方文明的交流。

"丝绸之路"：分为陆上丝绸之路和海上丝绸之路。"陆上丝绸之路" 是连接中国腹地与欧洲诸地的陆上商业贸易通道，形成于公元前2世纪—公元1世纪，直至16世纪仍保留使用，是一条东西方之间进行经济、政治、文化交流的主要道路。"海上丝绸之路" 是古代中国与外国交通贸易和文化交往的海上通道，主要以南海为中心，所以又称 "南海丝绸之路"。"海上丝绸之路" 形成于秦汉时期，发展于三国至隋朝时期，繁荣于唐宋时期，转变于明清时期，是已知的最为古老的海上航线。

Zhang Qian (164 BC —114 BC) was an outstanding diplomat, traveler, explorer and pioneer of the Silk Road in the Han Dynasty of China. Zhang Qian made two expeditions to the Western Regions successively, which opened the north–south road to the Western Regions of the Han Dynasty, namely the famous Silk Road. Zhang Qian was honored as "the pioneer of the Silk Road", "the first Chinese who opened his eyes to see the world" and "the Columbus of the East". He spread the culture of Central China to the Western Regions, and introduced Akhal teke horses, grapes, alfalfa, pomegranates and flax to Central China. His expeditions promoted the exchanges between eastern and western civilizations.

The "Silk Road" : including the land Silk Road and the maritime Silk Road. The land Silk Road is a trade channel linking China and the European countries, formed in the 2nd century BC to the 1st century AD, still used until the 16th century, is a main economic, political and cultural exchange between the east and the west. The maritime Silk Road is a maritime passage between ancient China and foreign trade and cultural exchanges, mainly centered in the South China Sea, so it is also called the Silk Road of the South China Sea. The maritime Silk Road was formed during the Qin and Han Dynasties and developed during the period of The Three Kingdoms Period to the Sui Dynasty. It flourished during the Tang and Song Dynasties and was transformed during the Ming and Qing Dynasties, known as the most ancient sea route.

> **我希望通过这次"熊猫小记者"的活动，让国外的友人们进一步了解中国的历史文化。**

I hope that through this "little panda reporters" news report project, foreign friends know more about China's history and culture.

岳城宇

10岁

成都四川大学附属实验小学西区

蓉欧快铁多像欧亚"陆上桥"

我是张骞队的"熊猫小记者",主要采访波兰、捷克、奥地利三个国家。临行前,我详细了解了西汉张骞出使西域的故事,被张骞不畏艰险、开辟丝绸之路的精神深深震撼。

2017年8月4日,我们登上飞往波兰华沙的国际航班。从这里开始,我们注定要经历一段不寻常的旅程。

▲在居里夫人故居前合影

蓉欧快铁:蓉欧国际快速铁路货运直达班列的简称,是跨国性质的运输工具。它自成都青白江集装箱中心站出发,经宝鸡、兰州到新疆阿拉山口出境,途经哈萨克斯坦、俄罗斯、白俄罗斯等国,直达波兰的罗兹站,线路全长9826公里,其中成都至阿拉山口3511公里、阿拉山口至罗兹6315公里。

在华沙,我们参观了居里夫人故居,向这位伟大的物理学家致敬。在华沙老城,我们看到美丽的和平鸽在墙上停留,在天上自由飞翔。

在参观哈特兰斯物流基地时,我们在众多的产品中发现了一个来自成都的箱子。工作人员说,"是通过蓉欧快铁运过来的,里面很可能是电脑配件"。工作人员告诉我们,**蓉欧快铁**被称为"铁轨上的丝

▲"熊猫小记者"采访中国驻捷克大使馆文化参赞吴光

绸之路",从成都出发,终点站就在波兰第二大城市罗兹。它将中国制造的货物运输到这里分散包装,然后快速分拨到欧洲其他地区,同时,波兰的优质产品也通过蓉欧快铁源源不断地运往中国。我们还了解到,来自成都的机械配件在欧洲很受欢迎,因为"成都造"质量很可靠!我不禁暗自高兴,为中国产品点赞!为成都加油!

告别波兰,我们来到捷克。中国驻捷克大使馆的文化参赞吴光阿姨告诉我们,中国与欧洲的联系越来越紧密,尤其是成都到捷克首都布拉格的直航开通后,越来越多的捷克人到成都旅行,参观大熊猫,也有越来越多的成都人飞到布拉格旅游,在广场喂和平鸽。"布拉格已经有成都火锅店啦!"她说。

9天的行程,我们进过许多超市、加油站,里面可以看到很多的

中国小商品，很多超市里还可以看到熊猫玩偶！特别令人惊奇的是，在奥地利维也纳金色大厅外面，我们还发现了一座熊猫雕塑！

回到成都，我一想到中国的商品在欧洲大受欢迎，心里就非常自豪。其实，我们还有很多的发展成果！在"一带一路"倡议的推进下，通过沟通欧亚的"陆上桥"——蓉欧快铁，一定能让世界分享到我们更多的发展成果！

小贴士

中国小商品：指中国的生产点多面广、品种花样繁多、消费变化迅速、价值相对较低的小百货，包括小五金、某些日常生活用品以及部分文化用品等。

▲捷克布拉格古城堡 （摄影 郇新华/视界）

Eurasian Continental Bridge High-speed Train between Europe and Chengdu

Yue Chengyu （10 years old, Affiliated Primary School of Sichuan University, West Campus）

I am one of the "little panda reporters" of Zhang Qian Team in this project. We covered the story of three countries: Poland, Czech and Austria. Before I left, I had a detailed understanding of the story of Zhang Qian in the Western Han Dynasty, and I was struck with Zhang's persistence of overcoming difficulties and explore the Silk Road.

On August 4, 2017, we boarded on international flight to Warsaw, Poland. From here, we are to go through an extraordinary journey.

In Warsaw, we visited Madame Curie's former residence and paid tribute to the great physicist. In the old city of Warsaw, we saw beautiful peace doves sitting on the wall or flying freely in the sky.

During a visit to the Hartland logistics base, we found a box from Chengdu in a number of products, which, according to a staff member, "is probably a computer accessory". This staff member also told us that the high-speed train between Europe and Chengdu is known as "the Silk Road on the rails", starting from Chengdu to Lodz, Poland's second largest city.

China-made goods are being shipped and distributed quickly to other parts of Europe, while Poland's quality products are being shipped to China through high-speed train. In the interview, we also learned that mechanical parts from Chengdu were very popular in Europe, because the quality was very reliable! I was very happy. Thumb up for Chinese products! Cheer for Chengdu!

Leaving Poland, we came to the Czech Republic. In the Czech Republic, we had the honor to interview officials in the Chinese embassy. From Madam Wu, the cultural counsellor, we learnt that Chengdu, connect more and more closely with Europe, especially after direct flights opened between Chengdu and Prague, capital of Czech. A growing number of Czechs travel to Chengdu to see the giant panda, and more and more people from Chengdu fly here to travel and feed the dove on Prague square. "There are Chengdu hotpot restaurants in Prague!" She said.

From the nine-day trip, I felt China was closely connected with Europe. For example, we passed by many of the supermarkets, gas stations, inside one could see a lot of Chinese small commodities, especially panda dolls! In particular, we found a panda sculpture outside the Golden Hall of Vienna, Austria.

Back to Chengdu, I am very proud to think that Chinese goods are so popular in Europe. In fact, there are many achievements of development other than that! Under the Belt and Road initiative, through communication with the Eurasian Continental Bridge high-speed train between Europe and Chengdu, we will surely share with the world more of our development achievements!

" 希望这次张骞队的行程中，我可以向欧洲朋友分享中国的优秀文化，让他们喜欢中国、喜欢成都！

I hope that through this journey, I may share China's excellent culture with my European friends, and China and Chengdu may win their favor! **"**

刘昱含

10岁

成都四川大学附属实验小学西区

我们的成都 世界的风采

2017年暑假，我很幸运地成为成都市广播电视台的"熊猫小记者"，参与全球追访"一带一路"大型公益新闻接力行动，心里别提有多高兴了！

成都是一座喝喝茶、看看戏、品尝数不胜数的美食、摆摆"龙门阵"的悠闲城市。成都也是一座流淌着文人墨客的清韵和风骚才子的惆怅的历史文化名城。古有诗云："成都海棠千万株，繁华盛丽天下无"；"晓看红湿处，花重锦官城"。成都的美景，远比赞美它的诗词丰富得多。

那三千年前的金沙太阳神鸟，那饱含追思的杜甫草堂，那雄伟的三国圣地武侯祠……令多少人魂牵梦绕，更不用说那风光旖旎的青城山、凝聚千年智慧的都江堰、憨态可掬的国际名片**大熊猫**、蜀味儿浓郁的宽窄巷子、浪漫多情的琴台故径……让成都获得了"休闲之都""美食之都""最佳旅游城市""宜居城市"的美誉。正如一位名人所说：成都，是一座来了就不想走的城市！

为当好合格的"熊猫小记者"，我们还带了很多特色礼物：憨厚可

小贴士

大熊猫：哺乳动物，体长约1.5米，外形像熊，尾短，体色为黑白两色，有着圆圆的脸颊、大大的黑眼圈、胖嘟嘟的身体。大熊猫已在地球上生存了至少800万年，是中国特有物种，现存的主要栖息地是中国四川、陕西和甘肃的山区。成都市区有成都大熊猫繁育研究基地，从事大熊猫的繁育和研究。

▲在安联足球俱乐部与捷克小朋友合影

爱的大熊猫玩具、**变幻莫测的川剧脸谱、金沙遗址出土的**
"太阳神鸟"图等。

　　经过10多个小时的飞行，我们终于来到波兰的华沙。
在瓦津基公园（又称肖邦公园），我们欣赏了郁郁葱葱的
树林、美丽的鸽子、错落有致的喷泉，还有可爱的小松鼠

小贴士

　　川剧脸谱：川剧脸谱
是川剧表演艺术中重要的组
成部分，是历代川剧艺人共
同创造并传承下来的艺术瑰
宝。脸谱是川剧的特色。在
川剧中，各种类型、各种人
物、各种表情有不同的脸
谱，分别代表不同的角色和
他们的喜怒哀乐。

小贴士

　　金沙遗址：在成都西郊
发现的古蜀文化的遗址，距
今3000年，反映商代晚期
至西周时期文明，展示了神
秘的古蜀文化和独特的青铜
文明。出土有古代象牙、金
器、玉器及神秘的"太阳神
鸟"金饰，现建有金沙遗址
博物馆。

小贴士

　　"太阳神鸟"金饰：出土于四
川成都金沙遗址，呈圆环状，器身极
薄。图案为镂空形式，分内外两层，
内层分布有12条旋转的齿状光芒，外
层有4只神鸟，首足前后相接，围绕着
旋转的太阳飞翔，中心的太阳向四周
喷射出12道光芒，体现了远古人类对
太阳及鸟的崇拜，是古蜀国黄金工艺
辉煌成就的代表。

呢！我们唱起了英文歌曲 *Little Star*，美妙的歌声消除了语言的隔阂，传递着来自中国的友谊。

我们一边向路人、游客散发宣传资料，一边微笑着介绍中国成都。不少当地人都涌过来与我们合影。其中一位老太太好奇地走过来，我立即微笑着迎上去，用我"椒盐味"的英文向她介绍道："遥远的东方，有个美丽的城市叫成都，欢迎您来做客。"老太太高兴地点头，并竖起大拇指说："good，good！"

在捷克、在奥地利，每到一处，我们都向世界各地的陌生人发出邀请，邀请他们到成都做客，到成都过春节，感受贴春联、串门、包饺子、吃汤圆、逛庙会等中国春节传统习俗。

▲在奥地利约翰·施特劳斯塑像下合影

Show Chengdu to the World

Liu Yuhan (10 years old, Affiliated Primary School of Sichuan University, West Campus)

In the summer of 2017, I was honored to be as a "little panda reporter" of Chengdu Radio and Televison Station to participate in this public welfare news relaying project and report on the Belt and Road initiative with other little reporters from Chengdu to all around the world . How happy I am!

Chengdu is a leisure city. Local people are fond of drinking tea, watching operas, tasting countless delicacies and living a carefree life. Chengdu is also a famous historical and cultural city with the charm of literati and the charm of the poet. There is a poem like this: "Millions of Haitang flowers (Chinese flowering crabapples) in Chengdu, prosperous and marvelous beyond the world." "In the morning one may see red flowers in Brocade City, bright colored by raindrops." And yet, Chengdu scenery is far more beautiful than what the poem describes.

The phoenix of Jinsha site three thousand years ago, Du Fu's thatched cottage which was filled with the memorial of Du Fu the poet, the magnificent Wuhou shrine of Three Kingdoms Period... many people cherish the memory, not to mention the scenic Mount Qingcheng and

Dujiangyan Irrigation System, which condensed ancient people's wisdom, the cute giant panda which is like a international card of Chengdu, charismatic Narrow and Wide Alley, romantic Qintai Site...Chengdu has won the reputation of "leisure capital", "food capital", "best tourism city" and "livable city". As a famous person said, Chengdu, is a city that people are reluctant to leave!

In order to be qualified "little panda reporters", we also brought a lot of special gifts, such as lovely panda toys, colorful Sichuan opera facial masks, golden sun bird replicas of Jinsha site, etc.

After more than ten hours of flying, we finally arrived in Warsaw, Poland. In the Lazienki Park (also known as Chopin Park), we enjoyed the lush forests, the beautiful pigeons, the scattered fountains and the lovely little squirrels. We sang the English song *Little Star*. Our song broke the language barrier and expressed our goodwill as chinese people.

We handed out introductory materials to passers-by and tourists, smiling and introducing Chengdu, China. A lot of local people came to take photos with us. When an old lady came over curiously, I immediately came up with a smile, and said to her with my Chinglish : "In the far east, there is a beautiful city called Chengdu, welcome to visit." The old lady nodded happily and gave me a thumbs-up, "good, good!"

In the Czech Republic, in Austria, everywhere, we invited foreign strangers to visit Chengdu, to celebrate the Spring Festival in Chengdu, to experience Chinese New Year traditional customs, such as sticking couplets on the door, paying visit to relatives, making dumplings, eating *Tangyuan*, and going to temple fairs, during the Spring Festival.

66 我想借"熊猫小记者"活动，宣扬中国文化，开阔视野，拓宽知识面，给国际友人留下一个良好的印象。

To be a "little panda reporter", I wish to promote Chinese culture, broaden my horizon, enrich knowledge and make a good impression on friends from all over the world. **99**

王新智

11岁

成都市华林小学

走进中国
驻捷克大使馆

大使馆：一国在建交国首都派驻的常设外交代表机关。大使馆代表整个国家的利益，全面负责两国关系，其首要职责是代表派遣国，促进两国的政治关系，其次是促进经济、文化、教育、科技、军事等方面的关系。同时，大使馆还具有领事职能。

大使馆，一个神圣的名词，它是一个国家在海外的国家象征，是旅居海外的人的心灵依靠。

embassy

中国大使馆是我无数次梦想去的地方，没想到，我的梦想很快就成真了。作为"熊猫小记者"的我，在2017年8月8日走进了中国驻捷克大使馆会客室，采访了中国驻捷克大使馆官员——吴光参赞。采访正式开始了，我有些忐忑地开始了我的记者工作。

▲ 采访活动

　　"吴参赞，您对中国的'一带一路'倡议有何见解和期望呢？"

　　吴参赞先是夸我说："这个小朋友很厉害哦，提出了这么高深的问题！"然后，她耐心地回答了我的问题。听着吴参赞详细的讲解，我更加觉得自己的祖国伟大！

　　在与吴参赞的访谈中，我了解到："一带一路"是连接沿线国家的纽带，也是祖国与沿线国家共同发展的契机。

　　我们还被特许参观了大使馆，这里陈列了许多中国各地的风光、民俗图片，还有许多新中国成立68周年的照片。在异国他乡看到这些图片，我感到更加亲切和温暖。

▲参观中国驻捷克大使馆

Into the Chinese Embassy in Czech Republic

Wang Xinzhi (11 years old, Chengdu Hualin Primary School)

The embassy is a place abroad symbolizes a country, a spiritual sanctuary for people living abroad.

The embassy is a sacred place I have dreamed of many times. My dream came true soon. As a "little panda reporter", I got the opportunity to walk into the reception room of the Chinese embassy in the Czech Republic on August 8, 2017, and interviewed the official of the Chinese embassy, counsellor Wu Guang. My heart beat fast. The interview began.

"What are your views and expectations on the Belt and Road initiative?"

"This kid is brilliant," Madam Wu said, "he asked such a good question!" Then she patiently answered my question. Listening to Wu's detailed explanation, I felt that my country was so great!

In the interview with Madam Wu, I learned that the Belt and Road initiative is the link between countries along the routes, and offers opportunities for the development of our country and countries along the routes.

In the embassy, many pictures of China's scenery, folklore and many photos of the 68th anniversary of the founding of the People's Republic of China were on display. Seeing these pictures in a foreign country makes me feel cordial and warm.

欧洲那么远，我想去看看！

**Europe is so far away,
and I wish to have a look!**

张子彦

12岁

成都市和平街小学

我送给欧洲的礼物

2017年暑假，我有幸成为成都市广播电视台的一名"熊猫小记者"，参与全球追访"一带一路"大型公益新闻接力行动。

那我该带点儿什么礼物去交流呢？爸爸一回家，我便急切地问："爸爸，什么东西能代表成都的特色呢？"爸爸反问道："你说呢？"我脱口而出："大熊猫！"爸爸笑着说："再想想，还有哪些能代表成都呢？"我挠挠后脑勺，一时答不上来。爸爸坐下来慢慢地讲道："成都是一座历史悠久的文化名城，有很多东西都是独特的，比如都江堰和青城山、蜀锦、蜀绣、银杏和芙蓉花、川剧和火锅等。但这些又怎么能作为礼物呢？"我和爸爸用了大半天时间，挑出了两

小贴士

蜀锦：专指蜀地（四川成都地区）生产的高级丝织提花织锦。蜀锦多用染色的熟丝线织成，用经线起花，运用彩条起彩或彩条添花，用几何图案和纹饰相结合的方法织成。

小贴士

芙蓉花：又名"木芙蓉"，为锦葵科、木槿属落叶灌木或小乔木。花于枝端叶腋间单生。芙蓉花是成都市市花，其花语为纤细之美、贞操、纯洁。

小贴士

蜀绣：又名"川绣"，是在丝绸或其他织物上采用蚕丝线绣出花纹图案的中国传统工艺，主要指以四川成都为中心的川西平原一带的刺绣。最早见于西汉，当时的工艺已相当成熟，其图案配色鲜艳、形象生动、富有立体感。

小贴士

银杏：银杏出现在几亿年前，是第四纪冰川运动后遗留下来的裸子植物中最古老的孑遗植物。现存活在世的银杏稀少而分散，和它同纲的所有其他植物皆已灭绝，所以银杏又有"活化石"的美称。同时，银杏也是成都市的市树。

川味火锅

样既能代表成都特色，又方便携带的礼物。我选的是一套色彩鲜艳
的川剧变脸小玩偶，俏皮可爱；爸爸选了一个蜀绣熊猫双面屏风摆
件，古朴精致。我想，这两份礼物一定会让外国朋友爱不释手。

　　8月8日，我们来到了捷克的罗德尼采小镇，这里有一个安联旗
下的足球俱乐部，这里也是欧洲很多足球俱乐部的训练基地之一。

　　面对足球高手，自然要学点儿技能！俱乐部的教练耐心地教我
们传球、带球、射门……尽管有点小笨拙，但我们踢得很认真。随
后，我们和当地的"足球小子"们进行了一场足球比赛。因为我们
好多"熊猫小记者"今天都是第一次真正意义地踢足球，所以……
结果您也许猜到了，唉，我们输了。

输了就输了，这也是交流。我把川剧变脸小玩偶送给了一个褐发碧眼、文静可爱的小男孩，他是守门员。他非常高兴，这套玩偶很快成了大家关注的焦点。翻译给他们解释道："川剧变脸是中国四川非常知名的传统表演，没有任何掩饰，瞬间就会换一张脸谱，而且可以连续变换多达十几张不同的脸谱，比魔术还神奇。"这些外国小朋友发出"哟哟"的惊叹声。

▲在安联足球俱乐部合影

我们将蜀绣熊猫双面屏风摆件赠送给足球俱乐部。俱乐部工作人员很兴奋，说会将这个来自中国成都的礼物摆放在俱乐部，让更多捷克人了解中国，了解成都。

My Gift to Europe

Zhang Ziyan（11 years old, Chengdu Heping Street Primary School）

In the summer vacation of 2017, I had the honor to be a "little panda reporter" of Chengdu Radio and Television Station to participate in this global news relay and report on the Belt and Road initiative with other small reporters from Chengdu.

As a "panda reporter", which kind of gift should I bring with me? As soon as dad came home, I asked eagerly, "Dad, which kind of gift can represent the characteristics of Chengdu?" Dad asked, "What do you think?" I blurted out, "Giant panda!" Dad smiled and said, "Think again, what else can represent Chengdu?" I racked my brain but couldn't answer it. Dad sat down and said slowly to me: "Chengdu is a famous cultural city with a long history. There are a lot of unique things, such as Mount Qingcheng and the famous Dujiangyan Irrigation System, the Shu brocade and embroidery, the ginkgo and hibiscus flowers, Sichuan opera and hotpot, and so on. But how can these be gifts?" My dad and I spent half a day picking out two gifts that were both of Chengdu style and easy to carry. I chose a set of colorful small dolls with Sichuan opera face masks, very cute indeed; dad chose a Sichuan double-sided embroidery panda screen, which was simple and delicate. I thought these two gifts, together with Shu embroidery, the colorful panda and other small gifts, prepared by the sponsors, would definitely impress foreign friends.

On August 8, 2017, in the morning, I arrived Roeder Nietzsche Town in Czech with my gifts. There is a soccer club affiliated with Allianz. In this town one of the major European soccer club training bases is also located.

Surely we would learn a lot from these soccer talents! The club coach took us to the field and taught us how to pass, dribble, shoot...Although someone was a little clumsy, everyone played very hard. Then we had a soccer match with the local kids in this club. Because many of our "little reporters" were playing soccer for the first time, so...As you might have guessed, alas, we lost.

It didn't matter. We still felt very happy. I gave the little Sichuan opera doll to a little boy with brown hair and blue eyes. He was the goalkeeper. He was very happy. The doll quickly attracted all attention. Interpreter explained to them: "Sichuan opera facial mask change is a very famous traditional performance of Sichuan, China, that is, without any disguise, the actor change a face in a moment. This performance may

be as many as a dozen of different continuous transformation of faces. It's more magical than magic." The kids gave an exclamation of "yo yo".

We presented the double-sided Shu embroidery panda screen to the soccer club members. They said they would display the gift from Chengdu in the club, so that more Czechs would know about China and Chengdu through this exquisite work.

> **读万卷书，行万里路，请跟随我们一起沿着张骞的足迹看世界！**
>
> Read ten thousand books and travel ten thousand miles. Please follow us along Zhang Qian's footsteps to see the world!

王蓝菲

11岁

成都市锦江外国语小学

与捷克小朋友的足球友谊赛

足球是我比较喜欢的一项体育运动，通过这次"熊猫小记者"行动，我有幸接触到专业的教练和训练，使我对足球有了更深的了解，知道了更多踢足球的技巧。例如，头球的正确部位只能是前额骨的正面和侧面。同时，根据顶球前的准备动作不同，又可分为原地顶球和起跳顶球。而起跳又分为单脚起跳和双脚起跳。根据球来的方向，又分为向前、向后和向两侧顶球……

▲安联足球俱乐部教练亲自教授足球技巧

在捷克上足球课时，我们和捷克的小朋友们都专心训练，一丝不苟地学习教练教的每一个动作。上了一会儿课，教练说要举行一场友谊赛，让我们"熊猫小记者"和捷克的小朋友比一比。我想：和他们比，

我们一定能赢，他们只有七八岁，年纪那么小，我们平均年龄要大一些，怎么可能输？

足球比赛开始了，球员们你追我赶，互不相让。足球就像个小孩子一样，一会儿跑到这儿，一会儿跑到那儿；一会儿跑到这个球员的脚边，一会儿又滚到那个球员的脚下，十分调皮。我在场上紧盯着足球，生怕它一不小心就滚到了对手的脚下。我方守门员双眼紧盯着在双方脚下变换的足球，他时前时后、时左时右，不停地变换着自己的位置。突然，足球飞了过来，守门员飞扑过去。可惜，足球从他身边擦肩而过，捷克的小朋友们进球了。

足球比赛结束后，我们问教练："教练，您怎么看这次活动？"教练回答道："这次活动非常好，不仅让孩子们多多交流，还促进了中欧友谊。很棒！"

捷克足球俱乐部之旅圆满结束，这次行程正体现了"一带一路"倡议秉持的理念：增进友谊，相互合作，让国家与国家之间达到共赢。我想，"一带一路"倡议，不仅是中国国家层面的外交行动，而且需要我们每个人的参与。

最后还想说一句：中国足球，加油！

Soccer Match with Czech Kids

Wang Hanfei (11 years old, Chengdu Jinjiang Foreign Language Primary School)

Soccer is one of my favorite sports. In the Czech Republic, I was lucky enough to get in touch with professional coaches. During the training, I gained a deeper understanding of soccer and more playing skills. For example, the heading is to use the front and side of the forehead. According to the preparation action the header can be divided into standing header and flying header which includes single foot jump and double-foot jump. According to the direction of the ball, it can be divided into forward, backward, and two sides...

During the soccer lesson, we were all tried very hard to followed every move of the coach meticulously. After a brief instruction, the coach said that there would be a friendly match between "panda reporters" and the Czech kids. I thought we could win. They were only seven or eight years old, compared with them, we were older on average. How could we lose?

The soccer game was on, the players were chasing the ball. The ball was like a naughty child, running here and there. Now and then it ran to the foot of one player or another. I stared at the ball, worrying that it would roll over to the foot of my opponent. Our goalkeeper closely watched the ball and he was constantly adjusting his position when he moved back and forth. Suddenly, the soccer flew over and the goalkeeper flew over. Unfortunately, he missed the ball, and the Czech kids scored.

After the soccer game, we asked the coach, "Sir, what do you think of the event?" The coach replied, "It's marvellous. Children got the chance to see the world, this event will surely enhance the friendship between China and Europe. Great!"

This is exactly the idea adhering to the Belt and Road initiative: enhance friendship and win-win cooperation of countries along the Silk Road. I think the Belt and Road initiative is more than a national diplomatic strategy. We are all involved.

Finally, I would like to say: Chinese soccer, come on!

成都是熊猫王国，我是"熊猫小记者"，随我一起出发，向世界宣传美丽的成都吧！

Chengdu is the kingdom of giant panda, I am the "little panda reporter". Let us go and show the beautiful Chengdu to the world!

杨祖懿

7岁

成都市泡桐树小学天府校区

让梦想绽放在维也纳金色大厅

维也纳金色大厅是维也纳最古老又最现代化的音乐厅，被誉为"世界五大音乐大厅之一"。我有幸来到了这座著名的世界音乐殿堂，在它宽敞的怀抱里聆听美妙的音乐，在它古雅的风格中感受艺术天才的演奏。

爸爸曾对我说，维也纳金色大厅是一个能让人安静下来的地方，当

时我不能理解。当我坐在金色大厅里，注视着音乐女神雕像时，我激动的心情真的自然而然地平静了下来。音乐响起，乐音袅袅，久久回响，让我沉醉。这是一个神奇的地方，它有一种魔力，深深地吸引着我、感染着我。一个小小的梦想在我心里开始萌芽。

我从小一直练习**古筝**，我很喜欢这门乐器，它让我深深地感受到了艺

小贴士

古筝：中国传统乐器中的筝乐器，属于弹拨乐器，是中国独特的、重要的民族乐器之一。它的音色优美，音域宽广，演奏技巧丰富，具有相当强的表现力，深受人们的喜爱。

　　汉服：汉民族传统服饰，又称"汉衣冠"、汉装、华服。其衣领有交领、圆领、对襟直领等；衣襟为右衽；衣袍用衣带、隐扣结系；衣袖长短宽窄皆有。主要特点是平面剪裁，下身较宽，系带。

　　唐装：中国的一种服饰，指唐制汉服，特征是交领、右衽、系带、无扣或布扣。代表有齐胸襦裙、唐圆领袍、交领襦裙等。

术的魅力。在金色大厅里，我想，如果能在这里听一曲古筝，那该多好啊！那柔和端庄的**汉服、唐装**，那时尚典雅的抚琴姿态，那清新脱俗的悠扬琴声，一定能征服这里的观众，东方文化一定会绚丽地绽放在金色大厅。如果我能在金色大厅演奏，那将会是什么样子呢？妈妈说，只有成为音乐大师，才能在这里表演。妈妈的话激励着我，也坚定了我练好古筝的信念。天才出于勤奋，只有通过勤奋练习，我才能提高自己的古筝演奏技艺，才能实现到金色大厅演奏的梦想。

　　今天，我是"熊猫小记者"，长大以后，我要成为文化使者，让自己的梦想绽放在维也纳金色大厅。

▲在奥地利的"快闪"活动

Cherish My Dream in the Golden Hall of Vienna

Yang Zuyi（7 years old, Paotongshu Primary School, Tianfu Campus）

The Golden Hall of Vienna is the oldest and yet interior modern concert hall in Vienna. It is honored as one of the top five music halls in the world. I had a chance to come to this world's famous music hall, listen to the wonderful music, enjoy the performance of artistic genius in this spacious hall with grace.

My father once told me that the Golden Hall of Vienna was a tranquil place. At the time, I couldn't understand his words. Today, as I sat in the Golden Hall, watched the statue of the music goddess, I felt peaceful inside. The music echoed in the hall, and the lingering sound got me drunk. This is a magical place. It has a magic, deeply attracted me. I was moved greatly. A little dream began to sprout in my heart.

I have been practicing ancient Chinese instrument—Guzheng since I was a child. I like this instrument very much.

It makes me deeply feel the charm of art. In the Golden Hall, I thought, if I could listen to the sound of Guzheng here, how wonderful it would be! The soft and dignified Han costume and Tang suit, the fashionable and elegant posture, the pure and beautiful sound, all of these surely would win the heart of the audience here. The Golden Hall would bore witness to splendid oriental culture. If I could play in the Golden Hall, what would it look like? Mom said that only if one became a master of music, he or she would be able to perform here. My mother's words inspired me and confirmed my determination to keep on practicing and pursue the dream of becoming the master of Guzheng. Only through diligent practice can I improve my skill and fulfill my dream.

Today, I am a "little panda reporter". When I grow up, I want to be a cultural ambassador, and cherish my dream in the Golden Hall of Vienna.

> 我是"熊猫小记者"，请跟着我们感受一路阳光！

I am a "little panda reporter". Please follow us to feel the sunshine on the way!

陈香羽

9岁

成都市泡桐树小学

不平凡的采访

2017年暑假，我有幸参与了成都市广播电视台"熊猫小记者"全球追访"一带一路"大型公益新闻接力行动。

我们张骞队"熊猫小记者"的采访，开始于波兰罗兹市的蓉欧快铁终点站。在罗兹，我们参观了很大的货物仓库，里面有各种各样来自世界各地的货物。我好奇地问库管阿姨："这么多货物里，有成都运过来的货物吗？"阿姨说："有啊，外面刚好还有一个集装箱，就是从成都装运过来的货物呢！"这是一批从成都运来的电器元件。蓉欧快铁开通后，从成都运过来大量这样的货物，比如汽车零部件、电子产品等，很受当地人的欢迎。

在罗兹的铁路客运大厅，我们向代表罗兹市政府来与我们会面的官员莫妮卡阿姨提了很多问题。

我问："您喜欢大熊猫吗？"

▲接受波兰国家电视台采访

　　她说："很喜欢大熊猫啊！我知道四川成都有大熊猫的自然保护区，可惜，我还没到成都看过真实的大熊猫呢。"

　　我问："那您知道有彩色的大熊猫吗？"

　　莫妮卡阿姨很惊奇："啊？真的吗？可能吗？"

　　哈哈！我们从成都带来了一只漂亮的彩绘大熊猫，正好可以送给她。这只彩绘大熊猫是我们从成都带过来的礼物，莫妮卡阿姨惊喜地说，这可是她的第一只"大熊猫"呢！

　　我们问莫妮卡阿姨："您知道'一带一路'吗？"

　　她说："当然知道啦。'一带一路'是一个伟大的倡议，波兰是'一带一路'沿线上的国家，罗兹也是在'一带一路'倡议中受益的城市。你们已经去过货运仓库，感受到了这种互相的交往和发展。我们政府很重视、很支持'一带一路'倡议呢！"

　　我作为一名"熊猫小记者"，圆满完成了采访任务。还有一个小秘密，我也是接受采访最多的小记者。记得当时波兰国家电视台的记者叔叔现场问了我一个问题："你长大以后想不想当记者？"

我说："想！"

"为什么呢？"

我认真地想了想，说："因为我觉得当记者可以了解不同的文化，也可以更多地了解其他国家的一些情况……"

中央电视台的记者叔叔曾问过我："以你自己的观点，怎么理解'一带一路'？"

我说："能让其他国家和中国共同发展，互相沟通交流，能了解相互更多的文化，能建立更好的友好关系……"

"熊猫小记者"这个称号，让我主动开始学会去认真地思考、慢慢地理解……我很自豪，我们是"熊猫小记者"，希望我们的团队一直团结下去。让我们一路阳光！共同成长！

▲接受中央电视台波兰站记者采访

An Unusual Interview

Chen Xiangyu (9 years old, Chengdu Paotongshu Primary School)

In the summer vacation of 2017, I had the honor to participate in public welfare news project "little panda reporters" of Chengdu Radio and Television station and report on the Belt and Road initiative.

The interview started at the European–Chengdu high–speed railway terminal in Lodz, Poland. In Lodz, we visited a very large warehouse with all kinds of goods from all over the world. I asked the lady in charge of the warehouse curiously, "Are there any goods from Chengdu?" She said, "Yes, there just arrived one container from Chengdu." It was a batch of electrical components shipped from Chengdu. After the opening of the high–speed railway, a large number of goods, such as auto parts and electronic products, were shipped from Chengdu, which was popular among local people.

In the passenger hall at Lodz station, we spoke with Monica, the officer who represented Lodz government. She

graciously answered our questions.

"Do you like pandas?" I asked.

She said, "I love pandas! I know there is a panda reserve center in Chengdu, Sichuan province, but unfortunately, I haven't seen the real pandas in Chengdu."

I asked again, "Do you know of pandas with color?"

Monica was surprised, "Huh? Is it true? Is it possible?"

Haha, this time we brought a beautiful painted giant panda doll from Chengdu, and we could give it to her. The painted giant panda doll is a gift selected from Sichuan local folk handicrafts which include Shu brocade and paper-cut. Monica said with surprise that it was the first "giant panda" she received!

We continued to ask Monica, "Do you know the Belt and Road initiative?"

She said: "Of course I do. It is a great initiative. Poland is the country along the Belt and Road, and Lodz is a city that has benefited from the Belt and Road initiative. You've been to the warehouse, and you've seen this kind of interaction and development. Our government supports and attaches great importance to the initiative."

I accomplished the interview with success as a "little panda reporter". Tell you a little secret. In this news relaying operation, I was also the most frequent interviewed little reporter. I remember one question raised by a reporter from

Polish TV, "Do you want to be a journalist when you grow up?"

I said, "I do!"

He asked, "Why?"

After careful consideration, I answered, "Because I think journalists can better understand different culture and also other countries..."

The reporter from CCTV asked me, "How do you understand the Belt and Road initiative in your own opinion?"

I said, "The initiative is a way towards friendship and common development by enhancing mutual understanding and strenthening communication..."

This title of "panda reporter" inspired me to learn to think seriously and gradually understand...I was very proud that we were "little panda reporters" and hope that our team will continue to unite. Let's go under the sunshine! Let us grow together!

> 不登高山，不知天之大；不临深谷，不知地之厚也。我是"熊猫小记者"，跟我去看更广阔的世界！

If you don't climb up high mountains, you will not comprehend the highness of the heavens; if you don't look down into a deep valley, you will not know the depth of the earth. I am a "little panda reporter", come with me to see a wider world!

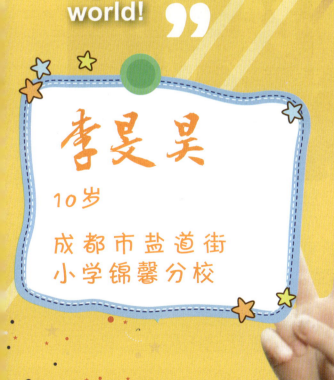

李旻昊

10岁

成都市盐道街
小学锦馨分校

一次游历，让我更爱家乡

　　2017年暑假，我有幸入选"熊猫小记者"啦！我们来到罗兹，这是蓉欧铁路货运专线的终点站，也是我们采访的第一站。在罗兹市郊的哈特兰斯物流基地，高大的仓库里有许多货架，分类摆放着琳琅满目的货物。通过蓉欧铁路运来的货物就在这里配送，我们发现有来自中国成都的集装箱。

▲在华沙郊区的物流基地寻找"成都造"

　　我们问工作人员："这些集装箱都是从成都运输来的货物吗？"他们很高兴地回答道："这个集装箱就是随着蓉欧快铁的班列抵达罗兹的，目前货物已通过汽车配送出去了，装载的是成都制造的机器配件。成都生产的零部件质量非常好。成都和罗兹都有一些装配工厂，部分来自中国的配件就在罗兹组装。"

　　罗兹市政府贸易发展和国际交流部主任莫妮卡女士向我们介绍了中国与波兰，特别是成都与罗兹之间的交流与合作。莫妮卡女士告诉我们：这趟专列对两地的发展非常重要，也给两地提供了一个交流的机会，从中国运过来的主要是电子产品和机械零部件，从罗兹运到成都的主要是一些农产品。

　　突然，莫妮卡女士问我们："成都有一个**大熊猫自然保护区**，那么，你们知不知道保护区里有多少只熊猫？"对这个问题我们却齐呼"不知道"。看来，作为小记者的我们，要补的功课还不少呢！

▲向世界推介成都

小贴士

　　大熊猫自然保护区：国家为了保护大熊猫而划定的特定区域。当前，我国设立了13个大熊猫自然保护区。

　　9天的行程中，我与很多外国小朋友进行了简单的交流。我发现，"国宝"大熊猫是成都最亮丽的名片，许多外国朋友都很喜欢大熊猫，也通过大熊猫知道了四川、知道了成都。

After the Journey, I Love My Hometown all the More

Li Minhao (9 years old, Yandao Street Primary School, Jinxin Campus)

In the summer of 2017, I was lucky enough to be chosen as a "little panda reporter" and arrived in Lodz, Poland. Lodz is the terminal station of the freight train and our first destination. At Hartlance logistics base on the outskirts of Lodz, there were a large amount of various goods on rows of shelves in tall warehouse. The goods transported by the railway were delivered here, and we found that there were containers from Chengdu, China.

As soon as we arrived, we interviewed the staff here, "Are these containers shipped from Chengdu?" They said, "This container arrived in Lodz along with European–Chengdu high–speed railway train. At present the goods have been delivered out by truck. The goods are mechanical accessories made in Chengdu. The quality of the production is very good. Both Chengdu and Lodz have some assembly plants, and parts from

China are assembled in Lodz."

Lady Monica, director of trade development and international communications at Lodz introduced to us a lot about the exchanges and cooperation between China and Poland, especially between Chengdu and Lodz. Monica also told us that this train was very important for the development of both, and also provided both side a chance to exchange. The products from China mainly included electronic products and components; and the products from Lodz to Chengdu were mostly agricultural products.

Suddenly, Monica asked us, "Chengdu has a panda reservation center, so do you know how many pandas are there in the reservation center?" It's a question! We all said, "We don't know." It seemed that as a small journalist, we had a lot of homework to do.

During the nine-day trip, I communicated with many foreign kids briefly. I found that our "national treasure" giant panda was the most beautiful card of Chengdu. Many foreign friends like the giant panda, and also know Sichuan and Chengdu through the giant panda.

❝ 追随张骞的足迹，做中外文化友好的使者。

Follow Zhang Qian's footsteps, and act as a cultural envoy of friendship. ❞

孙 欣

14岁

成都市棕北中学
科院校区

东欧游记

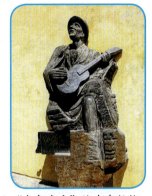

▲捷克布拉格城市风光 （摄影 刘杰/视界） ▲"金色城市"捷克布拉格 （摄影 刘杰/视界）

2017年暑假，我参加了"熊猫小记者"全球追访"一带一路"大型公益新闻接力行动。我沿着古代丝绸之路，追随张骞的足迹，带着对异域的期待，开启了东欧之行。

8月5日，我们来到了居里夫人的故居。居里夫人的故事我早有耳闻，她发现的镭元素为人类探索原子世界的奥秘打开了大门，用于医疗拯救了成千上万的癌症患者，但居里夫妇放弃了镭的专利权，是有崇高科学精神的科学家。当她的丈夫皮埃尔·居里去世后，居里夫人强忍悲痛，继续进行科学研究，努力造福人类。

LOVE

▲在居里夫人故居认真记录

8月7日，我们经过广袤的波德平原，来到了捷克共和国首都布拉格。在库特纳霍拉老城，我们参观了**圣芭芭拉教堂**，这是一座美轮美奂的哥特式建筑，是世界上最壮观的教堂之一。

▲ "金色城市"捷克布拉格 （摄影 刘杰/视界）

这次东欧之行，我一方面感受到了欧洲的文化，同时也领略了欧洲的饮食习惯与中国的差异。最突出的差别就是欧洲人好喝冷水，而我们喜欢喝热水。8月6日早晨，我因喝了两杯冷牛奶而拉肚子，可当

小贴士

圣芭芭拉教堂：捷克形状最特殊最漂亮的新哥特式建筑，1380年开始修建，直到20世纪才陆续完成。它与布拉格旧城堡中的圣维塔大教堂并列世界最壮观的教堂，其内部有金碧辉煌的天顶画。

▲在捷克人骨教堂

地人一年四季都喝冷牛奶。后来，我适应了那里的饮食习惯，试着像欧洲人一样吃饭。切猪排时，我切得手抽筋，但还是面不改色：优雅也是欧洲人的习惯。还有一天中午，我吃鸡排，刚吃了一半，转身倒水，结果盘子被收走了。原来，我摆错了**叉子的位置**，使侍者误以为我已用餐完毕。想当年，张骞在饮食习惯上会遇到多少困难呀。

小贴士

刀叉的摆放：西方进食的餐具，其摆放是有讲究的。刀叉在盘子上放成汉字的八字，刀刃朝内，不能朝外，叉子是弓朝上、齿朝下，这就是告诉服务生和别人，我这个菜没吃完。如果刀叉并排，刀刃朝外、叉齿朝上，代表的意思就是不吃了，可以收掉。

▲捷克温泉小镇 （摄影 刘杰/视界）

此次东欧之行，尽管我们还是一群孩子，但是我感受到了被采访者对我们的重视。一路的采访，不论在路上，还是在官邸或被访者家中，我们每次采访都特别有意义。采访对象给予了我们应有的尊重，他们没有因为我们是小孩子而敷衍我们，这让我们感到很温暖。这也许是我们身后有强大的祖国作支撑，也许是"一带一路"倡议得到当地人们的响应。作为"熊猫小记者"的我，将延续张骞的使命，做一名中外文化交流的使者。

Travel to Eastern Europe

Sun Xin (14 years old, Chengdu Zhongbei Middle School, Keyuan Campus)

In the summer vacation of 2017, I had the honor to be a "little panda reporter" of Chengdu Radio and Television Station to participate in this news relaying and reported on the Belt and Road initiative with other little reporters from Chengdu to all around the world. Along the Belt and Road, I followed the footsteps of Zhang Qian, started my journey to eastern Europe, full with the expectation to foreign lands.

On August 5, we came to Madame Curie's former residence. I have heard Madame Curie's story before. She has discovered the element of radium. The discovery opened the door for human to explore the mystery of the atom world. Its medical use saved tens of thousands of cancer patients. Then the Curies gave up the patent right of the radium. When her husband Pierre Curie died, Madame Curie bore her grief, and continued her scientific research. She worked hard for the benefit of mankind.

On August 7, we traveled through the vast Central European Plain to Prague, the capital of the Czech Republic. We visited the church of St. Barbara. Located in the old town of Kutna Hora, this wonderful church is a living history of the Catholic church, with its beautiful gothic look and glamorous glass windows.

Through the trip, I learn more about the European culture on the one hand; on the other hand, I knew more about the different diet habits between European and China. The most striking difference to me is that in Europe people drink cold water, and we Chinese prefer hot water. On the morning of August 6, I had two cups of cold milk and then had loose bowels, but the local people drink cold milk all the year round and feel okay. Later, I adapted to the diet habits there and tried to eat like Europeans. When I cut pork chops, I felt my hands aching, but I kept calm and went on with it. Elegance is also a typical European attitude. One day at lunch, while having chicken steak, I turned around to get some water, then my plate was taken away. It turned out that I have the fork in the wrong position, causing the waiter to think that I had finished my meal. Thousands of years ago when Zhang Qian went to the West, he must have many problems like this due to different dietary habits.

During the journey, I felt that we were taken seriously by all interviewees, though we were still kids. We interviewed people along the way, either in their working places or in their houses. All interviewees were kind to us, their kindness warmed our hearts. Maybe it's because our motherland is getting stronger, or because the Belt and Road initiative has won the responses and support of the local people. As a "little panda reporter", I will carry on Zhang Qian's mission to be a Sino-foreign cultural envoy of friendship.

追风的孩子

谭礼群（张骞队"熊猫小记者"陈香羽的妈妈）

　　童年时，记得曾读过一首少儿小诗《风筝》："我像天上飞翔的风筝，父母的爱，是那根连接风筝的线……"是啊，父母养育和培养孩子的过程，就像是放风筝的过程；孩子对于父母而言就像放飞的风筝，飞得再高再远，父母手中的线都拽得紧紧地不肯松开。从女儿开始上幼儿园起，我就一直在想，每一个孩子都有属于自己的世界，他们有自己的时代，终究会走上自己的道路的。我们父母能做的，便是在他们独自走向那条路之前，让他们拥有足够的"上路"和"在

路上"的能力。那么，这些能力应该包括哪些呢？

能想到的太多。有些事情，仅停留在内心的潜意识或直觉，会让人有些无所适从。就如你在划着一只小船，只知道一个大致方向，却不一定知道该如何奋力挥桨向着你心中企望的彼岸划过去一样……

然而，2017年夏天的不期而遇，却让我意外地豁然开朗。

这个"不期而遇"，便是女儿幸运地成为一名"熊猫小记者"，参加了成都市广播电视台组织的全球追访"一带一路"大型公益新闻接力活动。一次特殊的、顺应时势的、有意义的活动，能够让孩子快速地成长和收获。

在这个暑期之前，从女儿2岁至今的7年时间里，我一直坚持做着

同一件事：努力地尽己所能腾出一段又一段假期，带着一家老小满世界地去旅行。工作再忙，也会定期抽出时间计划我们的每一段自由行旅程。虽然并不完全清楚地知道自己的坚持到底给女儿的成长之路积累了些什么，但我相信"读万卷书、行万里路"总还是有道理的。女儿的见识、反应，在同龄孩子中还算不错，待人诚恳，比较开朗、大气。只是，这种对她而言纯粹的游乐和不需要太费脑筋的旅程多了以后，总是隐隐担心，在孩子的意识里，出门旅行会不会成为一种顺理成章的依赖和简单的娱乐享受？我们自己的旅程，是否又缺少了些什么呢？

曾经以为，这样的过程还会持续很久。"熊猫小记者"全球追访"一带一路"大型公益新闻接力活动的启动，让我快速地看到了很多改变。9岁，一个充满幻想、充满希冀和向往的年龄；"一带一路"，是我

们国家重要的发展构想和方向。这样风格截然不同的元素结合在同一个活动中，产生了神奇的"化学反

应"，充满了生命力。

这次"熊猫小记者"张骞队出访东欧三国的旅程，短短一个多星期，我欣喜地见证了很多"意想不到"。原本内心的忐忑不安被一个又一个的惊喜打破。这次活动，是女儿第一次真正意义上的独行，独自加入一个全新的团队去远行，"熊猫小记者"们都来自不同的学校。我们和孩子在短暂分离的过程中都在共同成长，一次真正的来自内心的成长。

"熊猫小记者"全球追访"一带一路"新闻接力活动举办的规模、号召力和影响力，让"熊猫小记者"这个称号在孩子的心里产生了使命感、责任感。责任感带来的内在力量，使她在面对独行的时候，比我们想象的更沉着淡定。我们更多看到的是她的积极行动、她发自内心的微笑。种种不

同于以往的主动表现，我们知道都是源于一种内心的自觉。这是一种我渴望已久的想在孩子身上看到的自觉。

伴随着活动启动仪式的成功举行，张骞队首先出发，我每天在中央电视台、成都电视台新闻频道、微信公众号"一头条"等新闻媒体上跟踪关注着活动信息，在这个过程中幸福感不断积累。这些喜悦和幸福感，体现在：

第一点，孩子学会了多方位思考。

比如，在参观学习的途中，每一处景点或场所她都有自己独立思考收获的心得，虽然是以孩子的视角，看似简单的"小道理"，但却也颇有意义。比如，在居里夫人故居、肖邦公园这些与名人有关的景点，通

过带队老师的介绍，她能意识到追求科学和艺术道路的艰辛，又能感叹于科技改变世界、艺术影响人们的生活，同时通过自己的思考，将其与"科技和文化传播"这些以前理解比较模糊的词语关联起来，真是令人惊喜。

又比如，在捷克，看到当地著名的提线木偶，她能马上想到自己家乡的皮影木偶、脸谱娃娃；在奥地利维也纳金色大厅听音乐会，看盛装的歌剧表演，能让她想到我们的京剧、川剧等艺术表演形式。从这种联想，再通过思考，她又能关联到各地特色产品的差异化和互通性，艺术表演的不同

和共性。

还有，在捷克与比自己团队年龄小的捷克小朋友们比赛足球，输了球能勇于承认自己球技确实不及对方，还能主动提出要学习对方的优点。

真是意想不到！孩子们眼中和心中收获的这些点点滴滴，不正是涉及我们"一带一路"倡议所提倡的"物质文明与精神文明的交流和互通"吗？孩子的这种思考方式，恰好也体现了"一带一路"倡议的理念之"互学互鉴"。

简单而顺其自然的思考过程，瞬间拉近了"一带一路"与孩子们的

距离。我想，孩子在路上冒出来的这种超乎我们想象的思维和思考，一定不是一蹴而就的。原因也是多方面的：孩子在学校接受的日常教育中，有学校和老师们越来越重视的素质教育做基础，加上电视台活动主办方和带队老师的专业引导，再加上孩子自身带着使命感认真地"上路"、用心地体验和感受……便产生了这些令我们惊喜的临场表现。而这种思考和思维方式，是未来所需要的，也是我们长久发展"一带一路"所需要的。孩子们会受益终生。

第二点，通过这次的活动，孩子们还收获了一个重要的礼物：团队精神。

在女儿的回忆中，"熊猫小记者"全球追访"一带一路"大型公益新闻接力活动的旅途中，无论碰上什么问题、麻烦，全程都有小伙伴们的团结互助，无论经历什么欢乐，小伙伴们也都共同分享。机场遇上航

班晚点，全队小朋友没有抱怨，自发地组织起来一起愉快地排练准备送给国际友人的合唱节目，以此忘却烦恼。会唱的小朋友主动地一个一个教不会唱的小朋友。在波兰罗兹参观和采访时，能为彼此出谋划策，实现团队内部合理分工，提问多样化、不重复，根据每个队员的特长分配任务，积极服从团队的安排。在维也纳面对街头宣传的任务时，共同积极准备，互帮互助练习英语……孩子们在一个团队中互相尊重、团结友爱。正因为这样，在短短的时间里，通过一路同行，通过面对每天新任务的挑战，"熊猫小记者"们结下了真挚的友谊，直至回到成都后都互相依依不舍，甚至有孩子回家后想到团队暂时分开了，伤心得快哭了。

孩子们的真性情，令人感叹。

"熊猫小记者"们通过这次活动实现的团队协同合作，其实不就是我们所理解的大局意识、协作精神和服务精神的集中体现吗？这也是"一带一路"倡议中提倡的"开放包容""共同合作"的体现。任何个体的力量都是渺小的，只有融入整体和团队，心往一处想，劲往一处使，才能实现真正的"互利共赢"。由小到大、由点及面，也许孩子们现在并没有意识到这么多，但是如果这份珍贵的礼物能陪伴着孩子们一路成长，如果身边的孩子们都能在成长的道路上收获到这份礼物，我们能看到的未来，一定是晴空万里、阳光明媚……

第三点，值得一提的，是孩子在这一次的旅程记录中让我最感动的一个细节：女儿说，在布拉格，他们来到了中国驻捷克大使馆，一踏上大使馆的红地毯，看到庄严的五星红旗，就像踏上了自己祖国的土地！

有点让人震惊，特别地让人骄傲！

我清晰地认识到，这次活动，真不是一次简单的参观、学习和看风景的旅行。孩子临行之前，我还以为，"一带一路"作为一个国家倡议，与一名小学生之间可能交集很少，连我们自己都一直还在学习的过程中。现在必须承认，我们真没有想到！孩子的旅程，也让我们有了收获。我们深刻地感受到，"一带一路"就在我们身边，与我们息息相关，如此具象化。面对中央电视台和国外电视台记者采访时，孩子们已经能够认真地用自己的理解来描述"一带一路"。当你越来越了解和理解它，你会越来越热爱自己的祖国并为之深深地感到骄傲和自豪。

……

2017年5月，在北京举办的"一带一路"国际合作高峰论坛恰似一阵春风，快速吹遍了大江南北，吹向了陆上和海上沿线国家和地区，吹进了每一个关心它的人的心里。这是整个时代的春风。

"一带一路"是宏大的事业，顺大势，必长久，会造福我们的世界。而"熊猫小记者"们，幸运地成为一群"追风的孩子"。

我们很诚挚地感谢成都市广播电视台，成功策划并给孩子们提供了这么好的机会，让他们参与这次特殊的"追风行动"。孩子参加这次活动，带给我自己的思考和收获，几乎打消了之前所有的无所适从。

我想，既然风来了，那么，让小风筝们顺着风的方向，飞吧！在慢慢放飞的过程中，他们会逐渐拥有和形成更适应飞翔的"骨架"：健康的身体，不断学习的能力，披荆斩棘的勇气，善良、真诚、包容、乐观、感恩的心，成熟的思考力、分析力和举一反三的能力，团结互助友爱的精神……

追风的孩子们，我们看见了：你们，在风中笑……

Wind Runner

Tan Liqun (Chen Xiangyu's Mother)

I remembered reading a little poem called *The Kite* in my childhood: "I am like a kite flying in the sky, my parents' love is the thread that holds the kite..." Yes, the process of raising and fostering children is like that of flying a kite. Children are like flying kites to their parents. No matter how high above or how far away, the lines of flying kites are still in their parents' hands. Since my daughter entered kindergarten, I have been thinking that every child has a world of their own. They enjoy their own time, and they will go their own way. What parents can do is to get them ready for going on the way alone. But how?

Too many things occur to me. The subconscious and intuitive thoughts may be be a little overwhelming. It's just like you are rowing a boat, though you know the direction, you do not know how to reach the other side.

However, the unexpected activity in the summer of 2017 inspired me in an unexpected way.

This "unexpected activity" was that my daughter was lucky

to be chosen as a "little panda reporter", and participated in the Belt and Road global news relaying sponsored by Chengdu Radio and Television Station. It turned out that a meaningful activity may help the child develop rapidly and gain a lot.

Since my daughter was two years old, in the later seven years, I've been trying my best to arrange trips with my family regularly despite busy work. While it's not entirely clear for me what should I do during the process of my daughter's growth, I still believe there's wisdom in the old Chinese saying: "Read a lot of books and travel a long way." My daughter's knowledge and experience is fairly rich among children of her age. She is sincere and open-minded. It's my concern that, after these kinds of easy pleasure trips, will she get used to simple entertainment? Is there anything missing in our journey?

I had thought that this travelling pattern would last for a long time. However, since the beginning of the global news relaying I found a lot of changes in my daughter in a short time. As a nine years old kid, she is full of imagination, hope and curiosity. On the other hand, the Belt and Road initiative is an important development initiative and direction of development of our country. Different elements meet together in this project, triggering a "chemical reaction", full of vitality.

The trip of little reporters of Zhang Qian Team to east Europe was just for over a week, and I was delighted to see a lot of surprises. Gradually, I put aside my concerns. The "little panda reporters" came from different schools. It was the first time for my daughter to go on a long journey with strangers by herself. In the short family separation, each of the family member became more mature.

The Belt and Road global news relaying exerted great influence on the "little panda reporter" in my home. The title itself evoked a sense of mission and responsibility in my child's heart, enabled her to stay calm while far away alone. More often we see her laugh out loud, more often we see her act positively. Different from her former behavior, we know that it is a passion from her inner heart that I have long wanted to see in my child.

The opening ceremony of the project held successfully, the starting story of Zhang Qian Team was covered every day on television news channel like, CCTV and Chengdu TV, on Wechat "Top Story" and other news media. We paid close attention to the coverage with happiness. We felt joyful because of following reasons.

First, the kids learn to think differently.

For example, during a visit on the way, she has her own independent thinking on each spot. The experience from a child's perspective seemed simple and minor, but it means a lot. At scenic spots related to celebrities, for example, in Madame Curie's former residence or in Chopin Park, through the introduction of the leader, she realized the hardship on the way to the pursuit of science and art. She understood that science and technology changed the world and the art exerted influence on people's lives. It was really amazing that she gained a better understanding of abstract words as "science, technology and cultural communication".

For example, in the Czech Republic, the famous local puppet immediately reminded her of the shadow puppet and face doll of her hometown. A concert in the Golden Hall in Vienna, Austria, and the opera performances, reminded her of our Peking opera, Sichuan opera and other artistic performances. Through thinking, she could also associate the differentiation and intercommunication of local specialty products and sum up differences and common points in art performances.

What is more, in the Czech Republic, when playing soccer with Czech kids who were younger than her, she had the courage to admit they were not good at the game and was willing to learn from others.

All of these were unexpected. Isn't it what the very idea of "communication and contact in material and spirit between different cultures" that the Belt and Road initiative for? This way of thinking also practiced one of the ideas of the Belt and Road initiative—mutual learning and mutual benefit.

It's a natural process for the children to think in this way. This way of thinking brought the Belt and Road closer to them. This process does not happen overnight. It comes from daily education in the school, quality-oriented education, TV broadcasts and teacher's professional guidance, combined with their own experience and feelings...And that's what surprised us. And this thinking mode is what we need in the future and we need to develop the Belt and Road for a long time. Children will benefit from it all their lives.

Secondly, through this project, the children also gained an important gift: teamwork spirit.

In the memory of my daughter, during the journey, whether confronted with problems or troubles, or experienced joy, all of the little reporters were helpful towards each other and willing to share weal and woe. When the flight was delayed, the whole team did not complain. They spontaneously organized and carefully rehearsed the chorus program prepared for international friends. The children who could sing actively taught the children who could not sing. In Lodz, Poland, they helped each other in travelling and interviewing, made reasonable planning with diversified questionnaires and arrangements of division and cooperation. Each team member was assigned to a task accordingly, and everyone was cooperative. In Vienna, when faced with the task of road show, they were eager to help each other practicing English...They showed respect and integrity in the process. It was precisely because of this, in a short period of time, through facing challenges of new tasks each day, during the journey the "little panda reporters"

became bosom friends. Until returned to Chengdu, they were reluctant to be apart from each other. Even when the children came home, they shed tears on the thought that the team members would be apart. How adorable they are!

In fact, the teamwork that the "little panda reporters" demonstrated through collaboration, is just such big words as overall situation consciousness, coherence spirit and service spirit and also the idea of "openness and tolerance" and "mutual cooperation" mentioned in the Belt and Road initiative. The power of each individual is limited, only when integrating into a whole, we can realize "mutual benefit and win-win policy". By collecting dots, perhaps unconsciously, with this precious gift, the children will have a bright future...

Third, what is worth mentioning is the most moving details that my daughter recorded in the journey. She said, in Prague, as they came to the Chinese Embassy in Czech, when she set foot on the red carpet at the embassy and saw the five-star red flag flying solemnly, she felt like setting foot on her motherland! I felt very surprised and was also very proud of her!

I realized clearly that this was not a trip for them simply to enjoy the scenery or to study or to pay a quick visit. Before her departure, I thought, the Belt and Road initiative may have little to do with kids, because this initiative was new to us adults as well. It must be admitted that the result is beyond our expectation. Through the children's experience, we were deeply aware that the Belt and Road is close to us all. In interviews with CCTV and foreign TV reporters, the children had been able to interpret the Belt and Road with their own words. The more you get to know and understand it, the more you will become proud of your country.

...

In May 2017, the Belt and Road Forum for international cooperation was held in Beijing. Like a spring breeze, it blew into people's hearts of each countries involved. This is the spring breeze of our time.

The Belt and Road is a grand cause. It will last long. It will benefit whole world. The "little panda reporters" fortunately became a group of "wind runners".

We sincerely thank Chengdu Radio and Television Station for successfully planning and providing the children with such a good opportunity to participate in this special wind running. After my child took part in this activity, I put aside my concerns and gained a lot.

I think, since the wind is coming, let's follow the wind, fly the little kites and keep them in the air! Fly the kites. They will gradually adapt to the fly and develop a robust "skeleton" including: a healthy body, learning ability, inner courage, sincerity, tolerance, optimism, a grateful heart, mature thinking, the analytical ability, teamwork spirit, love...

The wind runner, we see you flying and laughing in the wind...

"熊猫小记者"张骞队2018年夏季活动照片

◀7月31日在波兰华沙，听华为如何拓展欧洲市场

▲7月31日在波兰华沙参观华为区域总部，为中资企业点赞

▲7月31日在波兰华沙胜利广场

▲7月31日了解波兰华沙的中国商品

▲7月31日在波兰华沙一路认真看、认真听、认真记

▲8月1日在波兰大使馆与大使刘光源合影

▲8月1日在波兰罗兹与当地小朋友交流

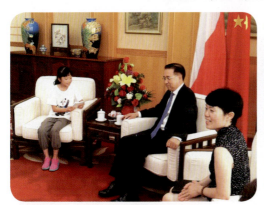

▲8月1日采访中国驻波兰大使馆大使刘光源，大使向熊猫小记者赠送礼物

▲经特许,8月1日在中国驻波兰大使馆爬树摘苹果

▲8月2日在罗兹市政府接受《罗兹日报》、TOYA电视台、新华社、人民网等媒体记者采访

▲ 8月2日"熊猫小记 ▶
　 者"在波兰刮起
　 "熊猫旋风"

◀ 8月4日在布拉格广场偶遇大熊猫

8月4日在捷克布拉格广 ▶
场唱响《成都》

▲ 8月6日在匈牙利金桥
中文学校，与当地学
生交流中文

8月6日在匈牙利金 ▶
桥中文学校写汉字

▲ 8月6日在匈牙利金桥
中文学校，与匈牙利
小朋友聊中文

第二章

马可·波罗队
新闻行动

Chapter Two
Marco Polo Team

马可·波罗 (1254—1324)

　　世界著名旅行家和商人。1254年生于威尼斯一个商人家庭，他的父亲和叔叔都是商人。17岁时，马可·波罗跟随父亲和叔叔前往中国，历时约4年，于1275年到达元朝的首都，与元世祖忽必烈建立了友谊。他在中国游历了17年，曾访问当时中国的许多古城，到过西南部的云南和东南地区，著有《马可·波罗游记》。

　　《马可·波罗游记》记述了马可·波罗在当时东方最富有的国家——中国的所见所闻，后来在欧洲广为流传，激起了欧洲人对东方的热烈向往，对以后新航路的开辟产生了巨大的影响。同时，西方地理学家还根据书中的描述，绘制了早期的世界地图。

Marco Polo (1254—1324) is a world-famous traveler and businessman. He was born in 1254 in a merchant family in Venice, and his father and uncle were businessmen. At the age of 17, Marco Polo traveled with his father and uncle to China for about four years. He reached the capital of China in Yuan Dynasty in 1275 and established a friendship with Kublai Khan, the emperor at that time. He stayed in China for 17 years and visited many ancient cities of China. He had been to southwest of China like Yunnan and southeast of China and wrote a book *The Travels of Marco Polo*.

The Travels of Marco Polo describes what Marco Polo saw and heard in the richest oriental country at that time—China. This book widely circulated in Europe later, stimulated the Europeans eagerly yearning for the East, which greatly motivated the opening of New Sea-route. At the same time, western geographers drew the early world map according to the description in the book.

66 大熊猫拉近了我与德国小朋友的距离。

The giant panda brought me closer to the German children. **99**

李佳忆

10岁

成都金泉小学

2017年暑假，我有幸成为"熊猫小记者"马可·波罗队的一员，前往德国、法国、意大利进行采访活动。

8月6日，我们来到了德国慕尼黑艺术中心。它是慕尼黑市区最具权威的多功能体验中心，不仅展示各种绘画艺术，还可以创作各种艺术作品。

▲宁芬堡 （摄影 刘杰/视界）

与德国小朋友共绘大熊猫

我对慕尼黑艺术中心的五彩绘画很感兴趣，也渴望能与国外的小朋友们进行艺术交流。随后，我们和当地小朋友进行艺术交流活动，我想，我既然来自大熊猫的故乡成都，大熊猫又是中国的"国宝"，我可以以大熊猫为主题进行创作呀！这样，既可以让当地小朋友了解大熊猫，也可以让

▲德国慕尼黑 （摄影 王达军/视界）

▲慕尼黑市政公园的雕塑 （摄影 刘杰/视界）

他们了解成都、了解中国呢。

于是，我迫不及待地和德国小朋友们一起画起了彩绘熊猫。为了让德国小朋友更好地认识大熊猫，我耐心地向他们描绘大熊猫有什么特征。大熊猫长得胖胖的，头圆圆的，尾巴很短，全身黑白相间，脸是白色的，耳朵和眼圈是黑色的。随后，我拿出了一个熊猫玩偶，送给了和我一起画大熊猫的德国小女孩。我向她介绍道："熊猫是中国的国宝，它的故乡在中国四川……"我的脑海里不断浮现出各种词语，一心想着如何让更多的德国小朋友了解熊猫，了解熊猫的故乡成都，了解中国。

▲向斯图加特电视台介绍成都是熊猫的家乡，是"一带一路"沿线的城市

我介绍时四周竟然站满了人，还有摄像机和话筒对着我！当手持话筒的记者叔叔对我说"谢谢"时，我才发现：呀！我在接受采访呢！瞬间，我感到些许害羞，但心里又充满兴奋，还感到一分自豪。这可是我第一次接受采访，而且还是在德国接受采访呢！我在德国让更多的外国朋友了解了中国、认识了成都。

Drawing Giant Pandas with German Children

Li Jiayi (10 years old, Chengdu Jinquan Primary School)

In the summer vacation of 2017, I had the opportunity to be a member of the "little panda reporters" of Marco Polo Team, participate in the global news relaying, go to Germany, France and Italy.

On August 6, we arrived at the Art Center in Munich, Germany. It is the most authoritative multi-functional experience center in the city of Munich. In the center, various styles of painting are displayed, various art works are also created.

I was very interested in the colorful paintings and eager to communicate with foreign kids. Then, while participating in art exchange activities with local children, an idea struck me. I thought, since I came from Chengdu, giant panda's hometown, and the giant panda was China's "national treasure", I could take the giant panda as a theme! In this way, the local children could learn about the giant pandas, and also knew about

Chengdu and China.

So I couldn't wait to paint the panda with the German children. In order to give German children a better understanding of the pandas, I patiently described to them: the giant panda is a very cute animal with round face and short fail. Its face is covered with white fur while its eyes and ears are covered with black fur. Later, I took out a panda doll and gave it to the little German girl who was painting the giant panda with me. I explained to her, "The panda is the national treasure of China, its hometown is in Sichuan..." English words kept coming up to my mind, I tried my best to get more German children to know about giant pandas, about Chengdu, the hometown of pandas, and about China.

I found myself surrounded by people with cameras and microphones during the introduction. When the person holding the microphone said "Thank you" to me, I realized: ah! I was being interviewed! Suddenly, I felt a little shy and excited, and this was my first interview, and I was interviewed in Germany! At the same time, I felt proud. I had let more foreign friends in Germany know about China and Chengdu.

" 期待中国的汽车也能像宝马汽车一样受到全世界人们的欢迎。

I wish Chinese cars to be as popular around the world as BMW is. **"**

高紫芊

11岁

成都玉林中学附属小学

德国宝马汽车博物馆里的"中国梦"

我作为一名"熊猫小记者"，于2017年8月6日来到了德国慕尼黑的宝马汽车博物馆。宝马汽车博物馆展示了不同时期、不同年代的各类宝马汽车，其中还有宝马摩托车。

▲宝马公司 （摄影 马川军/视界）

首先映入我眼帘的是一辆红色的老式宝马车，它的颜色非常亮丽。虽然它比我们现在看到的宝马汽车更加老式，但依然非常帅气。宝马汽车博物馆的楼梯非常独特，是螺旋形状的、纯白明亮的行道。我们沿着行道来到楼上，在一个半开放式的房间里，有许多白色小点在均匀移动，时不时会变化出一道道多姿多彩的风景线，像优雅的少女在整齐划一地跳着舞蹈。参观的游客纷纷拿出手机，拍下这美丽动人的风景。后来听了导游何老师的讲解，我才明白，那风景线是在演示宝马的造型和原理。

随后，我们走进宝马汽车博物馆的"历史走廊"。这里按出产年代排列着不同的宝马汽车，每一辆汽车都有自己

的"出生日期"，贴了型号标签，都有自己独特的风格呢。虽然有些汽车年代比较久远，可仍然光鲜铮亮、帅气十足。尽管我没有真正坐上去体验一番，但依然能感受到这些宝马汽车的迷人风采。

　　宝马汽车是德国的骄傲。据我所知，除了宝马，德国还有许多著名的汽车品牌。目前，中国有很多汽车是和德国合作制造的，还有许多汽车零部件用的是德国品牌或者欧洲其他国家的品牌。但是我相信，不久的将来，中国一定会出现像宝马汽车一样享誉世界的汽车品牌。我希望，下一次来欧洲的时候，将会看到更多的中国品牌、中国制造，不论是汽车、食品，还是家具……通过"一带一路"倡议，我觉得，中国已经朝这个目标迈进了一大步！我坚信，我这个"中国梦"一定会实现！

▲高紫芊向中国驻意大利大使馆新闻处主任张爱山送上熊猫玩偶，并介绍此行的收获

China Dream in BMW Museum in Germany

Gao Ziqian (11 years old, Affiliated Primary School of Chengdu Yulin Middle School)

As a "little panda reporter", I arrived at the BMW Museum in Munich, Germany on August 6, 2017. The BMW Museum shows various types of cars and motorcycles of BMW from different eras.

The first thing that caught my eye was a vintage automobile with a strong, bright red color. Although it was outdated, it still looked very handsome. The unique staircase at the BMW Museum is a spiral, pure white and bright walkway. Along the staircase we went upstairs, in a half opened room, there were many small white dot moving evenly from time to time, the colorful scenery looked like elegant girls dancing in unison. Visitors took out their smartphones and took pictures of the beautiful sight. After listening to the explanation of the guide, I realized that the movement of the dots was demonstrating the shape and manufacturing theory of the auto.

Then we walked into BMW Museum's historic corridor. There were different BMW cars in the sequence of the production years. Each car had its own "date of birth", and each model label had its style. Although some were vintage cars, they were still shiny and bright. Although I didn't actually sit in and experience it, I could still feel the charm of these BMW cars.

BMW is the pride of Germany. As far as I know, there are many famous automobile brands in Germany besides BMW. At present, many car manufactures in China are in cooperation with Germany, and many auto parts are made in German brands or other European brands. But I believe that in the near future, China will have a world-renowned car brand like BMW. I hope that the next time we come to Europe, we will see more Chinese brands or "made in China", whether it's cars, food, furniture...Through the Belt and Road initiative, I think China has taken a big step forward towards this goal! I firmly believe that my "China Dream" will come true!

" 我期待坐着中国高铁到法国旅行。

I'm looking forward to travelling to France by Chinese high-speed train. **"**

黄沚源

14岁

四川大学附属中学初中部

当我坐上法国高铁

2017年8月9日，我们从法国的斯特拉斯堡到马赛，体验了一次法国高铁。法国高铁平稳、快速。在高铁上，我们一行人吃了法国最传统的早餐——面包。面包颜色金黄偏黑，外壳脆硬，里面却酥松柔软，还夹着番茄、青菜和嫩肉……

我们坐在高铁上，沿途欣赏着法国的田园风光，每一处稻田，就如同一张明信片一般充满诗情画意。牛羊在草地上随意地吃草，远处的山脚下隐约可见一座座别墅。这些建筑看上去年代有点久远，却十分漂亮。

我突然冒出一个问题，法国的高铁与中国的相比，哪个更好呢？

我了解到，法国的铁路事业发展较早，拥有的高铁数量居欧洲第一，但是法国高铁造价高昂。而中国铁路造价相对较低，速度快，票价也低，性价比高，可谓后来居上。法国和中国的高铁都十分平稳，据

说，在列车启动或刹车时，容器盛满的水都不会溢出来呢。

我想，古丝绸之路上的商人们都是用马匹将自己的商品运往各地，既费时又费力，而现在只需坐在舒适的座位上，欣赏着窗外风景或者美美地睡上一觉，就到达目的地了，多方便呀！

在法国的行程中，我们在家乐福超市还看到了不少中国制造的产品。我不禁猜想，它们是通过飞机、轮船还是火车到达法国的呢？随着"一带一路"合作的不断推进，中国与欧洲国家的经济交流不断加强，我想，以后在法国看到的"中国制造"会越来越多。我真希望，将来能直接从中国坐高铁到达法国，那该多方便啊！

On the French High-speed Train

Huang Zhanyuan (14 years old, Affiliated Middle School of Sichuan University)

On August 9, 2017, we went from Strasbourg to Marseilles to experience high-speed train in France. France's high-speed trains run smoothly and fast. We had traditional French breakfast—bread. The bread looked brown, tasted tender yet crispy, with tomatoes, green vegetables and tender meat inside.

We sat on the high-speed rail and enjoy the idyllic scenery of France, each of which was like a scenic postcard. The cattle and sheep were grazing in the meadow. Dimly visible villas appeared here and there at the foot of the distant hill. These old buildings were very beautiful.

I suddenly wondered, which one was better, France's high-speed train or that of Chinese?

As far as I know, the railway industry in France has developed earlier, with the highest number of high-speed trains in Europe. But the cost of high-speed train in France is very high. China's railways are cheaper, but also faster and more effective. Both French and Chinese high-speed trains are so steady that when the train starts or breaks, the water in a container won't overflow.

I thought, the ancient merchants along the Silk Road had their goods shipped on horses, it's both time-consuming and inefficient. Now, all you have to do is to sit comfortably enjoying the scenery outside the window, or have a sound sleep, then you will reach the destination. How convenient!

During our trip to France, we also saw a lot of products made in China at Carrefour. I couldn't help wondering whether they arrived in France by plane, ship or train. With the continuous promotion of the Belt and Road cooperation, the economic exchanges between China and European countries have been continuously strengthened. I think more and more products "made in China" will appear in France. I'm looking forward to travelling to France by Chinese high-speed train. That would be so convenient!

> **期待更多的"中国制造"走出国门。**
>
> I wish more and more products made in China go abroad.

冉浥尘

8岁

成都市泡桐树小学天府校区

在法国寻找「中国制造」

马赛，这座有着2500年历史的古城，是法国第二大城市和最大的海港。很久以来，马赛就是东西方贸易往来的重镇，曾经在"海上丝绸之路"中扮演着重要角色。我们"熊猫小记者"于2017年8月9日来到了美丽的马赛。走在这座山丘环抱、景色秀丽、气候宜人的城市中，我想起了历史书上写的马赛人高唱战歌进军巴黎鼓舞人们为自由而战的情形……

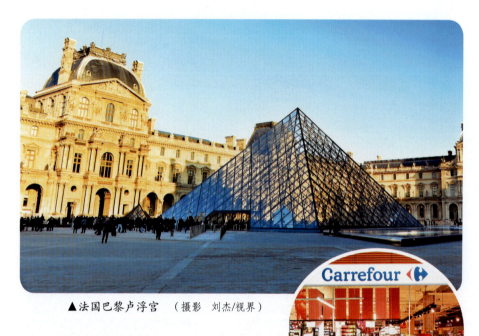

▲法国巴黎卢浮宫 （摄影 刘杰/视界）

领队王旭老师怎么带我们到了家乐福超市啊？哈哈！你要是以为我们来购物，那你就错了！告诉你吧，我们是在这里来寻"宝"的——寻找中国制造的商品。怎么样，挺新鲜吧？

小伙伴们分头寻找。经过一番查看，我决定发挥小记者的特长，采访一位超市工作人员。在简单的问候和自我介绍后，我向超市工作人员询问超市里"中国制造"的情况。我了解到，

这里的日常生活用品、服装玩具，大多"made in China"。我们一边聊一边找。难以置信！我竟然找到了青岛啤酒！接着，我听到有人大喊："花椒，花椒，这里有四川的花椒！"另外一边也传来了："我找到中国制造的鞋了！"每个人都充满了成就感。一想到"中国制造"与法国人民的生活息息相关，我就感到无比自豪！

▲法国巴黎 （摄影 王达军/视界）

离开家乐福超市，我们乘坐的大巴在法国的街道上行驶，路边不时有中国餐馆映入我们的眼帘，一会儿看到一家"四川火锅"，一会儿又出现一家"潮州餐馆"。每发现一家中国餐馆，都引来小伙伴们的阵阵惊呼。这些也是地地道道的"中国造"啊！

咱们中国正在从一个"制造大国"转变成一个"制造强国"！中国的商品通过各种渠道走向世界。"一带一路"倡议的实施，一定能让我们有更多的商品走出国门。"一带一路"倡议的合作，真正拉近了中国与沿线国家的距离。

通过这次活动，我们真真实实感受到了"一带一路"给世界带来的影响。我不禁陷入了沉思，作为一名小学生，我又应该怎么做呢？这时，耳边仿佛传来了同学们的诵读声："少年强则国强……"

Products Made in China in France

Ran Yichen（8 years old, Chengdu Paotongshu Primary School, Tianfu Campus）

Marseilles, a 2500-year-old city, is France's second largest city and the largest seaport. For a long time, Marseilles had been an important trade center between the East and the West, and had played an important role on the maritime Silk Road. Our "little panda reporters" arrived in beautiful Marseilles on August 9, 2017. It's a city surrounded by hills, with beautiful scenery and pleasant climate. While wandering about, I thought of the historic scene when Marseilles men marched into Paris, calling on people to fight for their freedom...

Why did Wang Xu the leader bring us to Carrefour? Ha ha! If you thought we were going to shopping, you'd be wrong! Let me tell you, we were here to look for "treasure" —to search for goods "made in China". How's that? Isn't it fancy?

My partners split up to search. After searching for a while, I decided to act as a real reporter and interview a supermarket worker. After simple greetings and self-introduction, I asked the supermarket worker about the origin places. I learned that most of the daily necessities, clothing and toys were made in China. We talked while looking for the goods. Unbelievable! I found Qingdao beer! Then I heard my partner shouting "Peppercorns, peppercorns, Sichuan peppercorns!" On the other side I heard "I found the shoes made in China!" Everyone was filled with a sense of achivement. I was very proud to think that products made in China were so closely related to everyday life of the French people.

After Leaving Carrefour, we took a shuttle bus in the French street. From time to time, there were Chinese restaurants catching our eyes. For a moment we saw a Sichuan hotpot restaurant here, over there a Chaozhou restaurant. Each time a Chinese restaurant was found, it attracted a lot of exclamations from us. These were also "made in China"!

China is transforming from a "big manufacturing nation" into a "powerful manufacturing nation"! Chinese goods go to the world through various channels. The Belt and Road will be a road for more goods to go abroad. The Belt and Road cooperation has really brought China closer to countries along the routes.

Through this project, we truly felt the impact of the Belt and Road initiative on the world. I could not help thinking, what should I do as a primary school student? At this time, the voices of my classmates seem to resound in my ears: "The stronger the youths are, the stronger the nation will be..."

> **❝** 欣赏着马可·波罗当年欣赏的美景，期待着"丝绸之路"万古长青。
>
> I wish the Silk Road forever young while enjoying the beautiful scenery that Marco Polo once enjoyed in his era. **❞**

王良国

14岁

成都七中育才学校水井坊校区

"丝绸之路"上的古城掠影

2017年8月10日，作为"熊猫小记者"的我来到了热那亚。热那亚是一个靠近地中海的港口城市，曾是一个历史悠久的城邦国，因海上贸易而繁荣，是"丝绸之路"上一个重要的节点城市。它为何能在"丝绸之路"上发挥重要作用呢？

首先，热那亚不但通水路，陆上交通也很便利。很早以前，海上运输还极不成熟，任何一个小风浪就可以置人于死地，而陆路相对安全，

所以最早的"丝绸之路"是从陆地打开的。热那亚曾属于罗马帝国。在汉代，罗马帝国被称为"大秦"，当时的中国人就知道它的繁荣与强

大。罗马帝国重视交通，频繁开拓陆上贸易，热那亚的经济贸易由此得到了迅速发展。

后来，随着航海技术的不断发展，海上运输也逐渐成熟。热那亚海上贸易频繁，经济实力逐渐强大，成为地中海地区的强国。许多载着东方贸易品的船只，都选择在热那亚港口停泊。

8月11日，我们来到了马可·波罗的家乡——著名的水城威尼斯。大巴到达港口，我们便转乘摆渡船到威尼斯本岛。

▲意大利威尼斯 （摄影 刘杰/视界）

走进威尼斯，我首先感受到的是一种历史的沧桑。贡多拉从百年历史的小砖拱桥下缓缓驶过，留下一道道悠悠的波纹。我静立在桥上，感觉自己与这个水上小城融为了一体。

意大利威尼斯 （摄影 郑良发/视界）

据介绍，这里的房子大多有500年至700年的历史，当年修建后就一直没动过，只不过是加了电线等生活必需物品。水面之上便是无漆的红砖，斑驳的墙体像一位历史的见证者，明明心中话语万千，却又只是默然无言。

我静静地欣赏着水城的美景，海天一色，群鸥化作白色的羽箭在海上穿梭，船只零星散布，悠悠摆动。想当年马可·波罗走出家门，即将踏上行程之时，也曾眺望过这番美景吧！他便觉得眼前的蔚蓝指引着未来开阔的世界，万千尽纳于胸，面对未知而神秘的东方，也不再有丝毫恐惧。犹如现在的"一带一路"倡议，它一定能不畏艰险，向前再向前，因为前方便是空旷的碧海与耀眼的光芒。

想到这里，我忽然很想知道，几千年后，"丝绸之路"又将是什么模样呢？

▲意大利威尼斯 （摄影 刘杰/视界）

The Ancient City on the Silk Road

Wang Liangguo (14 years old, Chengdu No.7 Yucai Middle School, Shuijingfang Campus)

On August 10, 2017, I came to Genoa as a "little panda reporter". Genoa, a port city close to the Mediterranean Sea, was once a city state with a long history. It thrived on maritime trade and was an important hub on the Silk Road. Why did it play an important role on the Silk Road?

First of all, Genoa is not only accessible by water, but also by land. Long time ago, sea transport was still very inconvenient, and a small storm could kill people. Land transport was relatively safe, so the earliest Silk Road was on land. At that time, Genoa belonged to the Roman Empire. In the Han Dynasty, the Roman Empire was called Da Qin, and the Chinese people knew it as a prosperous and powerful nation. The Roman Empire attached great importance to transportation and frequently explored land trade, thus the economy and trade of Genoa developed rapidly.

Later, with the continuous development of navigation technology, sea transport also gradually became convenient. Genoa became a great power in the Mediterranean region, with frequent maritime trade and growing economic power. Ships carrying oriental trading goods chose to berth at the port of Genoa.

On August 11, we came to Venice, Marco Polo's hometown, a famous city on water. When the bus arrived at the port, we took the ferry to the island of Venice.

Entering Venice, a strong sense of history greeted me. Gondola slowly passed under the centuries-old brick arch bridge, leaving a string of long ripples. I stood on the bridge, feeling myself in harmony with this city on water.

According to the introduction, most of the houses here have 500 years to 700 years of history. They remain the same after being built, except some maintenance of wires and other necessities. The scene of unpainted red brick above the water and mottled wall bear witness to the history. At this tranquil moment, stories of the splendid past seemed to being told in the wind.

I quietly enjoyed the beautiful scenery of the city on water, the sea melted into the sky, a flight of gulls shuttled above the sea like a white arrow, the scattered boat leisurely swung. When Marco Polo was about to start his journey, maybe he saw this beautiful scenery as well. He would feel that this blue sky was guiding to the future. Facing eastward towards the unknown and the mystery, he would feel full of encouragement and fear no more. Just as the Belt and Road initiative, it's a road leading us forward fearlessly into the future, because the broad blue sea and shining sky are lying waiting ahead.

Thinking of this, I am suddenly eager to know what the Silk Road would look like thousands of years later.

" 中国大使馆是身在异乡的中国人的家。

The Chinese Embassy is home for Chinese abroad. **"**

彭铃欢

10岁

成都市锦官新城小学

走进中国驻意大利大使馆

意大利的首都罗马是意大利的政治、经济、文化和交通中心，也是古罗马文化的发源地，是世界著名的历史文化古城。中国驻意大利大使馆就坐落在罗马。

▲意大利罗马斗兽场 （摄影 郑良发/视界）

▲意大利圣彼得大教堂 （摄影 郑良发/视界）

2017年8月13日，我作为"熊猫小记者"的一员，走进了中国驻意大利大使馆。馆内高大的树木郁郁葱葱，一面五星红旗在一片大草坪上迎风飘扬，格外鲜艳夺目。在五星红旗旁边有一对雕像，是古代中国的两位圣贤——孔子与老子。

大使馆的新闻处主任张爱山叔叔接见了"熊猫小记者"。我怀着激动的心情，代表

▲参观中国驻意大利大使馆

同学们给张叔叔送上我们从四川成都带来的卡通熊猫礼物。张叔叔高兴地接受了我们送给他的礼物，带领大家进入庄严而美丽的大使馆会议室。通向会议室的路上，铺着一条长长的红地毯，两旁是花岗石做成的石柱。地毯的尽头，左侧是代表中国文化的几十座大大小小的编钟，右侧是摆满了各种造型的瓷器和唐三彩的平台。在会议室门前的墙面上，悬挂着中国和意大利两国的国旗。

在大使馆会议室里，我问张叔叔：意大利人民喜欢熊猫吗？张叔叔说，全世界人民都喜欢中国的大熊猫，因为大熊猫象征和平，而我们"熊猫小记者"则是传播友谊与和平的文明使者。同学们纷纷向张叔叔提问，有的还提到了"一带一路"的相关问题，大家还谈了自己对此次

▲意大利米兰大教堂 （摄影 刘杰/视界）

▲意大利罗马比萨斜塔 （摄影 郑良发/视界）

活动及在国外宣传"一带一路"的心得体会与感想。张叔叔耐心地解答我们的问题，并且对我们的体会表示认同。

张爱山叔叔说，民心相通是最重要的也是最基础的，"熊猫小记者"活动促进了成都与欧洲国家青少年之间的交流，在沿线国家唱响中国民歌《茉莉花》与朗诵中国诗人杜甫的古诗《春夜喜雨》，这就是对古丝绸之路的传承与提升，唤起了历史的记忆，增强了沿线各国人民的相互尊重与理解、交流和沟通。

通过这次活动，我的独立思考能力有了提高。这次活动也让我对"一带一路"倡议有了更直接的感受，700多年前的马可·波罗加深了中意两国的友谊，

那友谊之花必将开得更加灿烂。

Into the Chinese Embassy in Italy

Peng Linghuan (10 years old, Chengdu Jinguan New City Primary School)

Rome, the capital of Italy, is the political, economic, cultural and transportation center of Italy and the birthplace of ancient Roman culture. The Chinese Embassy in Italy is located in Rome.

On August 13, 2017, I entered the Chinese Embassy in Italy as a member of the "little panda reporters". In the museum, tall trees were lush and green, a five-star red flag standed on a large lawn. Beside the five-star red flag, there was a pair of statues, which were the two saints of ancient China—Confucius and Laozi.

Ambassador Zhang Aishan, the director of the information office of the embassy, met with "little panda reporters". On behalf of my classmates, I gave Mr. Zhang a gift of cartoon panda from Chengdu, Sichuan. Mr. Zhang happily accepted the gift we gave him and led us into the solemn and beautiful embassy conference room. The way to the conference room was covered with a long red carpet, with granite pilliars on both sides. At the end of the way, on both sides there were art works on display. On the left, there were dozens of various chime bells of chinese style. On the right, there were porcelain and tri-colored glazed potteries. On the wall in front of the conference room, the flags of China and Italy were hung.

In the embassy conference room, I asked Mr. Zhang, "Do the Italian people like pandas?" Mr. Zhang said that people all over the world loved China's giant pandas because they symbolized peace. As "little panda reporters", we were messengers of friendship and peace. The reporters began to ask Mr. Zhang questions, and some questions were related to the Belt and Road initiative. We also talked about our experiences about the news relaying. Mr. Zhang patiently answered our questions and expressed appreciation to our experiences.

Mr. Zhang said, the core of the Belt and Road initiative was people-to-people bond. The "little panda reporter" project would promote the communication among teenagers in Chengdu and European countries. The activities of singing Chinese folk song *Jasmine* and reading Chinese poet Du Fu's poem *Happy Rain on a Sping Night* evoked memories of history, strengthened mutual respect and understanding, exchange and communication with the people of all countries along the Silk Road. This was to inherit and sublimate of the ancient Silk Road.

Through this project, we became more mature, and my ability of independent thinking was improved. I understood more about the initiative. The friendship between China and Italy strengthened because of Marco Polo 700 years ago, and the flower of friendship will bloom more splendidly.

" 我也像马可·波罗一样，成为一名连接中国与欧洲的文明使者。**"**

I would like to be a goodwill messenger between China and Europe like Marco Polo. **"**

傅子萱

14岁

成都嘉祥外国语学校

不一样的沟通

　　2017年8月6日至13日，我作为"熊猫小记者"马可·波罗队的一员，有幸参与一场奇妙之旅，与外国友人进行了一次不一样的沟通。

　　"好一朵美丽的茉莉花，芬芳美丽满枝丫，又香又白人人夸……"悠扬的中国民歌《茉莉花》在德国新天鹅堡唱响，这是我们这群来自中国成都的"熊猫小记者"在这个全球最具人气的旅游胜地之一，送给来自世界各地的游客的礼物。缕缕幽香、淡淡洁白的花儿，在德国的土地上悄然绽放，人们纷纷驻足欣赏，并对我们报以友好的微笑和鼓励的掌声。

　　一位来自英国的父亲甚至拍摄了我们的表演，说要带回去给他的孩子看，让他的孩子通过歌声了解中国。当我告诉一对德国夫妇我来自中

▲新天鹅堡 （摄影 刘杰/视界）

▲参观中国驻意大利大使馆

国、来自成都的时候，这位名叫戴德的先生和他的妻子十分激动，居然用中文对我说"你好"。原

来，戴德先生曾经在中国工作，还去过成都！我给他们介绍了中国的"一带一路"倡议，介绍了成都的发展和变化。戴德先生觉得这个活动非常有意义，他认为"一

带一路"倡议提出后，德国和中国的合作会越来越多，他希望能进一步加强民间交流，期待能参与咱们全球追访"一带一路"第二季的活动，再次到成都做客……

在慕尼黑艺术交流中心，我把画好的大熊猫送给了一个可爱的小女

孩。当她得知我来自熊猫的故乡时非常羡慕。她爸爸说，等她长大后，会带她到成都的街头走一走。

在永恒之城罗马，我们受邀来到了中国驻意大利大使馆，新闻处主任张爱山叔叔接受了我们从家乡带来的具有成都元素的小礼物，并带我们参观了大使馆。我问了一个心里想了很久的问题：成都和意大利有没有经贸往来，体现在哪些方面？张叔叔回答说，意大利有宽窄巷子。这个消息着实让我们兴奋，宽窄巷子可是成都的标志性名片啊！看来，咱们成都的魅力棒棒哒！至于经济贸易方面的往来，他希望我们"熊猫小记者"将来能承担起沟通成都与意大利经济往来的任务，因为我们是连接中国与世界的文明使者……

这次不寻常的旅行、不一样的沟通永远刻在了我的脑海里，因为我也像马可·波罗一样，成了一名连接中国与欧洲的文明使者。

A Special Exchange

Fu Zixuan (14 years old, Chengdu Jiaxiang Foreign Language School)

On August 6, 2017, as a member of "little panda reporters" of the Marco Polo Team. I got the opportunity to participate in a wonderful journey, and I had a special communication with foreign friends.

"Jasmine, jasmine, oh so fair, fragrant and beautiful here and there, pure and fragrant all declare..." A melodious folk song *Jasmine* resonated at Neuschwanstein Castle in Germany, and this was presented by "little panda reporters" from Chengdu to the world's most popular tourist destinations for visitors from all over the world. Pure and fragrant flowers bloomed on this land quietly. People stopped, smiled and applauded warmly.

A father from England shot our performance and said he would take it back home and let his children learn about China by singing. I bravely came to a German couple. I told them in English that I was from China, from Chengdu. The gentleman named Dade and his wife were very excited, even said "hello" to me in Chinese. It turned out that Mr. Dade had worked in China and had been to Chengdu! I introduced to them the Belt and Road initiative of China, and introduced the development and change of

Chengdu. Mr. Dade thought this project was very meaningful. He thought that Germany and China would cooperate in more and more ways after the initiative being proposed, and people-to-people exchanges would be enhanced. He was looking forward to participating in our global news relaying in the second season, and coming to Chengdu once again...

At the Munich Art Exchange Center, I presented a painted giant panda to a cute little girl. She was very excited when she learned that I came from the hometown of giant panda. Her father promised that he would take her to Chengdu when she grew up.

In Rome the eternal city, we were invited to come to the Chinese embassy in Italy. Director Zhang Aishan accepted our small gifts of Chengdu style, and took us to visit the embassy. I asked a question that had been on my mind for a long time: was there any trade between Chengdu and Italy? Mr. Zhang replied that there was a Narrow and Wide Alley in Italy. This news really excited us. Narrow and Wide Alley is the icon and business card of Chengdu! See, Chengdu is so charming in Italian heart! As for economic and trade exchanges, he wished that in the future, the "little panda reporters" may endeavor to promote Italian economic exchanges with Chengdu, because we are messengers connecting China and the world civilization...

This special visit has embedded in my mind forever. Like Marco Polo, I would like to be a goodwill messenger between China and Europe.

" 我要像马可·波罗一样，做一名连接中外文化的友好使者。

I want to be a goodwill messenger of Chinese and foreign cultures like Marco Polo. **"**

吴睿霖

9岁

成都师范附属小学华润分校

追寻马可·波罗的足迹

2017年暑假，我有幸成为"熊猫小记者"，参加全球追访"一带一路"大型公益新闻接力行动，去追寻马可·波罗的足迹。8月6日，我踏上了德国的土地。那慕尼黑安联球场，从远处看，就像个巨大的橡皮艇。这座可以容纳7.5万人，以精巧的结构、壮丽的外观而著称的球场，成为慕尼黑以至于德国的荣耀。球场大到我无法用语言来形容。想象在里面举办球赛时的场景，我脑中顿时浮现出激烈比赛的现场，仿佛听到了球迷们排山倒海的呐喊声。作为一名小小足球爱好者，我的心不禁怦怦直跳。

然后，我们来到了宝马汽车博物馆，它建于20世纪70年代初期。在这里，我们了解参观了宝马汽车公司成长及发展过程中的各种车辆，让我们对这个汽车生产历史最悠久的国家产生了由衷的敬佩。

在新天鹅堡（也叫"灰姑娘城堡"）这个有着美丽、浪漫的爱情

▲在斯图加特与当地小朋友合影

故事的城堡前，我们为游客们演唱了中国的经典歌曲《茉莉花》，向他们介绍了熊猫之乡的"一带一路"的主题活动。

斯图加特是科技与历史相结合的城市，大名鼎鼎的奔驰、保时捷就诞生于这里。

8月9日，我们来到了法国的斯特拉斯堡。它位于莱茵河的西岸，而莱茵河的东岸便是德国。因此，斯特拉斯堡充分融合了法德两国的历史文化，歌德、莫扎特、巴斯德等名人都曾在这里居住。在这里，我感受到

▲意大利威尼斯圣马可大教堂 （摄影 邬新华/视界）

了历史文化与现代文明的碰撞。

　　8月11日，我们来到了水城威尼斯，它是马可·波罗的故乡。那曲折的水巷纵横交错。赏完美景，我们在圣马可广场上演唱《茉莉花》，吸引了很多游客，随后向他们介绍了"一带一路"倡议。我们也感受到了当地市民的热情、友善。

▲意大利佛罗伦萨　（摄影　王达军/视界）

　　艺术之都佛罗伦萨以美术工艺品和纺织品而驰名全欧洲，美术学院闻名世界，更是文艺复兴的发源地。这里处处呈现在眼前的都是古代艺术家们的杰作，充满了魅力，它的古典与优雅让我流连忘返。最后一站我们来到了中国驻意大利大使馆，送去了以代表和平友爱的大熊猫为元素的礼物。

Follow the Footsteps of Marco Polo

Wu Ruilin (9 years old, Affiliated Primary School of Chengdu Normal University, Huarun Campus)

In the summer vacation of 2017, I was lucky to be a "little panda reporter", and participated in the Belt and Road global news relaying. Following the footprints of Marco Polo, on August 6, I set foot on Germany. The Munich Allianz Arena, seen from a distance, looked like a giant rubber dinghy. The football stadium, with more than 75000 sitting capacity, was widely known for its magnificent appearance and delicate structure, and had become the honer of Munich and Germany. The stadium was so big that I couldn't describe it in words. Imagine the scene in which the game was held, and the scene of the fierce competition flashed into my mind, as if the fans were shouting at me. As a little soccer fan, my heart beat fast.

Then we came to the BMW Museum, which was built in the early 1970s. We caught a glimpse of the history of growth and development of automobile production. We couldn't help admiring the oldest car manufacturer.

At Neuschwanstein (also known as Cinderella Castle), I was a little excited to see the castle with a beautiful and romantic love story. In front of this ancient castle square, we sang the classic Chinese song *Jasmine* to the tourists and introduced the Belt and Road initiative to them.

Stuttgart is a city combined technology and history. The famous brand Mercedes Benz and Porsche were born here.

On August 9, we arrived in Strasbourg, France. It lies on the west bank of the Rhine River, and the east side of the Rhine is Germany. As a result, Strasbourg is fully integrated with the history and culture of France and Germany. Goethe, Mozart, Pasteur and other celebrities once lived here. I felt historical culture melt into modern civilization here.

On August 11, we came to Venice, the water city, the hometown of Marco Polo. The zigzag water lanes crisscross the flow. After enjoying the beautiful scenery, we sang *Jasmine* on Piazza San Marco. Our song attracted a lot of tourists. Then we introduced the Belt and Road initiative to them. We felt the warmth and friendliness of the local people as well.

Florence, the well-known art capital, birthplace of Renaissance, is known for handicraft and textile. The Academy of Fine Arts in Florence is world famous. It is full of masterpieces of ancient artists, and it is full of charm. I was fascinated by its classical and elegant style. At the last stop, we arrived at the Chinese Embassy in Italy and presented giant panda doll and handcraft as gifts. They represented peace and love.

" 我希望将来成为中德友谊的使者。

I hope to become a messenger of Sino-Germany friendship in the future. **"**

鲁佳颖

10岁

成都市高新区
益州小学

我的德国印象

我是马可·波罗队的一员，我们带着四件具有成都特色的礼物——原织蜀锦、彩绘大熊猫、中国剪纸、绳编，开启了一段奇妙的旅程。我们一共到了三个国家：德国、法国和意大利。其中，德国给我留下了深刻的印象。

8月6日，我们来到慕尼黑艺术中心，感受到德国是一个热爱艺术的国度，并且非常重视少儿艺术教育。当我走进艺术中心大厅，看到墙上挂着小朋友们各式各样的画作。这些作品想

象力丰富，非常富有创意。看到这些作品，我们不禁手痒痒了。在老师的安排下，我们与德国小朋友一起画画。在

画画中，我交了许多好朋友。尽管我们语言不通，但画笔就是一种通用的语言。

告别了慕尼黑艺术中心，我们来到了宝马汽车博物馆。如果说慕尼黑艺术中心体现了德国人的想象力，那么宝马汽车博物馆就体现了德国人的实干精神。那一辆辆不同时代的宝马车，在诉说着它们的辉煌。而今，宝马汽车还行驶在成都的大街小巷。一个具有百年历史的汽车品牌不断地焕发出新的

活力，我国作为汽车工业的后起之秀，是不是可以学点什么呢？

8月7日，我们来到安联球场，它是欧洲最现代化的球场。从远处看，球场像一只巨大的橡皮艇，白色椭圆体之外包裹着许多气囊样的结构，现代感十足，同时也给人强烈的视觉冲击。听说它能容纳7.5万名观众。最为神奇的是，在照明系统的映射下，安联球场会成为一个红色的发光体，几英里外都可以看到。在这里，我们还上了一堂足球课，德国教练教授了一些踢球的技巧。同时，我们还与德国一群八九岁的孩子举行了一场友谊赛。尽管他们都比我小，可是，踢球技术一点儿也不差，也许，这就是德国足球很强的原因吧。

新天鹅城堡又叫灰姑娘城堡，是迪士尼城堡的原型。听说，它的修建过程非常曲折，与一个凄美的爱情故事有关。爱看《格林童话》的我，被城堡的景色深深吸引。也许，灰姑娘仍然就在这城堡的某个地方……它带给我们无限的想象。

8月8日，我们来到威廉玛动植物园，它是欧洲最大的动植物园，建

于19世纪40年代。园内有1000多个不同品种的8000多只动物，我们可以通过围栏和玻璃房观赏到许多动物及植物。我们一路观看，一路听导游的讲解，我非常感慨德国人对动植物的关爱。

很快，我们就离开德国了，可是德国人的想象力、实干精神、足球、环保意识却永远留在了我的脑海里。我想，"一带一路"倡议不仅是商品交流的经济纽带，而且是相互学习的友谊桥梁。

▲ "熊猫小记者"接受采访

German Impression

Lu Jiaying (10 years old, Chengdu High-tech Zone Yizhou Primary School)

I was a member of the Marco Polo Team. We started a wonderful journey together with four gifts with Chengdu characteristics: the original Shu brocade, colorful painting of giant panda, Chinese paper cutting, and weaving cord. We came to three countries: Germany, France and Italy. I was deeply impressed by Germany.

On August 6, I came to the Munich Art Center, and I felt that the Germans love art and attache great importance to children's art education. When I walked into the hall of the art center, I saw all kinds of paintings on the walls. These works were imaginative and creative. Seeing these works, we itched to draw. Under the teacher's arrangement, we drew with the German children. In drawing, I made many good friends. The language barrier was not a problem. Drawing is a universal language.

Farewell to the Munich Art Center, we came to the BMW

Museum. The Munich Art Center embodies the German imagination, the BMW Museum embodies the German craftsmanship. The BMW cars of different eras show us their past glory in silence. You can see BMW cars on the streets of Chengdu. A century-old car brand is constantly revitalized. The car manufacturing industry in China is still developing. Is there anything we can learn from BMW?

On August 7, we came to Allianz Arena, the most modern stadium in Europe. From a distance, the stadium looks like a giant rubber dinghy. The white ellipsoid is surrounded by inflated plastic panels. The modern look of the stadium has big visual impact on audiences. It is said that it can hold 75000 people, and the most amazing thing is that, under the lighting system, the football stadium will become a red luminous body that can be seen a few miles away. We had a football lesson here, and the German coach gave us some instructions. At the same time, we had a friendly match against a group of eight or nine years old kids in Germany. Even though they were younger than me, their skills were not bad at all. Maybe that's where the German football strength lies.

Then we came to New Swan Castle, also called Cinderella castle, which is the prototype of the castle in Disneyland. It is said that the construction process is very complicated, and it relates to a beautiful love story. I was attracted by the view of the castle as a fan of the *Grimm's Fairy Tales*. Maybe Cinderella is still somewhere in the castle...It gives me infinite imagination.

On August 8, we arrived at the Wilma Zoological and Botanical Garden, Europe's largest park for animals and plants. It was built in the 1840s.There are now more than 8000 animals of over 1000 different species in the park. We saw many animals and plants through the enclosure and the glass house. We watched all the way, listened to the introduction of tour guide, and I was very impressed by Germans' love of animals and plants.

We left Germany soon, but the German's imagination and craftsmanship, their football skills, the awareness of environmental protection imprinted in my mind forever. I think the Belt and Road is not only the economic belt of commodity exchange, but also a friendship bridge of mutual learning.

新闻接力行动随想

唐艺铭（马可·波罗队"熊猫小记者"彭铃欢的妈妈）

　　1877年，德国地质地理学家李希霍芬在其著作《中国》一书中，把"中国与中亚、中国与印度间以丝绸贸易为媒介的这条西域交通道路"命名为"丝绸之路"。20世纪初，德国历史学家赫尔曼进一步确定了"丝绸之路"的基本内涵，即中国古代经过中亚通往南亚、西亚以及欧洲、北非的陆上贸易交往的通道。2013年9月和10月，中国国家主席习近平在出访中亚和东南亚国家期间，先后提出共建"丝绸之路经济带"和"21世纪海上丝绸之路"的重大倡议，得到国际社会高度关注。2015年3月，中国国家发改委、外交部、商务部联合发布了《推动共建丝绸之路经济带和21世纪海上丝绸之路的愿景与行动》，"一带一路"带着全新的使命再次登上历史舞台。

　　我们的"一带一路"也是世界的"一带一路",它不是历史上丝绸之路的再现或重建,而是前无古人的一项创举;它是中国人民对全世界人民的友好态度,是我们盼望世界和平的愿望;它承载着沿途国家的发展、繁荣与梦想,是全世界人民的开放之路、文明之路、创新之路、繁荣之路、和平之路。

　　2017年初夏,由成都市广播电视台、成都市妇联、国新智库文化发展中心指导,国家新闻出版广电总局国际合作司支持开展的全球追访公益新闻活动——"'熊猫小记者'全球追访'一带一路'接力行动"正式启动,德国、波兰、法国、新加坡驻蓉领事馆均派出代表参加了隆重的出发仪式。此次活动以少年儿童为主体,旨在传承与提升古丝绸之路,唤起历史记忆,增强沿线各国人民的相互尊重,理解、沟通与交流。

　　2017年8月,"熊猫小记者"分为张骞队、马可·波罗队与郑和队，分别沿三条主题线路出发，前往"一带一路"沿线国家开展活动。小记者们带着体现成都历史文化传承的蜀锦、彩绘大熊猫、传统剪纸、彩编中国结等伴手礼，怀揣着和平与友谊，向世界介绍成都，向全世界传播悠久灿烂的中国文化。

著名的近代儿童心理学家皮亚杰认为："教育的目的不仅仅是增加儿童的知识，而是为儿童设置智慧刺激的环境，让儿童自行探索，主动认知与学习。""熊猫小记者"全球追访"一带一路"大型公益新闻接力行动从策划到实施，每一个环节都充分体现了这一理论。"熊猫小记者"在紧张的行程中面对着不同国家、不同民族，观察、体验着不同的地域文化，这样国际化和多元化的环境，对每位在中国出生和成长的少年儿童来说，都是一次极其难得的文化交流与学习机会，也是一次完全陌生而又充满挑战的人生经历。

在慕尼黑少儿艺术之家，小记者们展示了自己的绘画才艺、手工制作技能、陶艺及硬笔书法，得到了慕尼黑少儿艺术之家老师们的赞誉；

在斯图加特市中心王宫广场，小记者们用流利的英语向当地的民众介绍了自己的家乡成都。74岁的德国老人西格弗里德·豪克在了解了孩子们此行的意义后，对孩子们的勇气和聪慧表示了赞赏。正如马可·波罗队领队、成都市广播电视台的王旭女士所说，这就是让同学们用自己的脚步丈量"一带一路"的壮阔之美，让他们亲身感受并传递沿线国家人民的深厚友谊。

教育是帮助认识发展的过程。在多元化的国际环境中，"熊猫小记者"自始至终都以主人翁的身份，用饱满的热情和友好的态度，走访、连接、宣传丝绸之路。无论是在德国安联球场的绿茵场上，还是在法国斯特拉斯堡，或是在风帆点点的马赛港；无论是在欧洲文艺复兴发源地的佛罗伦萨，还是在世界上国家最小却拥有全世界最大教堂的梵蒂冈，"熊猫小记者"们身体力行地告诉沿线各国民众，"一带一路"形成了相互理解、相互欣赏、相互尊重的人文格局，是全世界和平之路。

　　在中国驻意大利大使馆，新闻处主任张爱山代表大使李瑞宇接见了"熊猫小记者"们。张爱山主任耐心仔细地听取了同学们对走访、连接、宣传"一带一路"的心得体会与感想。"熊猫小记者"们向张爱山主任表示，这一路走来，不仅深刻理解了"一带一路"在全世界人民心中的意义，感受到祖国的强大，还磨炼与提升了自己的心理素质与思想境界，大家都做到了直面困难、克服困难、战胜困难，自理能力与独立思考能力每天都在增强。张爱山主任与小记者们交流时说："民心相通是最重要的也是最基础的。'熊猫小记者'活动促进了成都与欧洲国家青少年之间的交流。你们在各个沿线国家唱响中国民歌《茉莉花》与朗诵中国古诗词《春夜喜雨》，引起各国民众的极大兴趣与关注，沿线媒体追踪报道，这是加强古丝绸之路上各国文化交流实实在在的举动。"

　　古丝绸之路曾经跨越大陆和海洋，在人类文明史上书写了繁荣发展、文明交融的篇章。今天的"一带一路"犹如海陆双翼，助力中国发展，带动沿线国家共同繁荣。它的愿景与构想正在世界各国人民心中落

地生根，复兴丝绸之路这一幅横贯东西共谋发展的宏大蓝图正在铺展。

"一带一路"倡议，给全世界人民带来了无限生机和美好前景。"熊猫小记者"们正是在这样的历史背景下做出了自己责无旁贷的努力与贡献。"风声雨声读书声，声声入耳；家事国事天下事，事事关心。"这是当代青少年必须具备的素质；"天下兴亡，匹夫有责"，这是中国人民的决心；"天下兴亡，舍我其谁"，这是"熊猫小记者"们的抱负！"一带一路"是中国梦的具体化，我们有理由相信，沿着中国特色社会主义道路继续前进，我们一定能够实现中华民族伟大复兴的中国梦，世界和平之梦！

On the Project of the News Relaying

Tang Yiming (Peny Linhuan's Mother)

In 1877, the geographer Richthofen defined "Silk Road" in his book *China* as following: "the Silk Road was an ancient network of trade routes to the Western Region connecting China and central Asia, China and India with silk trade." At the beginning of the 20th century, German historian A. Herrmann further expanded the connotation of "Silk Road" as "the land trade routes connecting ancient Chinese through central Asia to south Asia, west Asia and Europe, north Africa". In September and October, 2013, Chinese President Xi Jinping, during a visit to central Asia and southeast Asia countries, successively proposed the initiative of the Silk Road Economic Belt and the 21st Century Maritime Silk Road, together referred to as the Belt and Road initiative. The Initiative immediately won a positive response from the countries involved. In March of 2015, *Vision and Actions on Jointly Building Silk Road Economic Belt and 21st-Century Maritime Silk Road* was issued by the National

Development and Reform Commission, Ministry of Foreign Affairs, and Ministry of Commerce of the People's Republic of China, thus the Belt and Road stepped onto stage of history once again with a new mission.

The Belt and Road is China's initiative, but it belongs to the world. It is not the reconstruction of the Silk Road in history, but an unprecedented innovation. It shows the Chinese people's friendly attitude towards people all over the world, and it shows our hope for world peace. It will bring development, prosperity to the countries involved. We will build the Belt and Road into a road of opening-up, a road of civilization, a road of innovation, a road of prosperity and a road for peace.

In early summer of 2017, Chengdu Radio and Television Station, Women's Federation of Chengdu, the Cultural Development Center of Guo Xin Think-tank, International Cooperation Department of State Administration of Press, Publication, Radio, Film and Television, co-sponsored the project of global news relaying on the Belt and Road by "little panda reporters". Representatives from consulates of Germany, Poland, France and Singapore in Sichuan Province attended the grand opening ceremony. This children-oriented activity was to instill vitality into the ancient Silk Road, cherish historical memory, and enhance mutual respect and understanding, communication among the peoples along the Belt and Road.

In August 2017, the "little panda reporters" were divided

into three teams: Zhang Qian Team, Marco Polo Team and Zheng He Team, went along three theme routes, and departed for countries along the Belt and Road. The little reporters carried four kinds of souvenirs with them: Shu brocade, chinese knot drawing of giant panda, Chinese paper-cut, Chinese knot, which were all with Chengdu characteristics. They would introduce Chengdu to the world, and spread long and splendid Chinese culture all over the world for peace and friendship.

According to the theory of the famous modern child psychologist Jean Piaget, the purpose of education is not only to increase the knowledge of children, but also set stimulating environment for children to explore and to learn through active cognition. The entire project of news relaying, from scheme to execution, is based on this theory. Each "panda reporter" somehow underwent culture shocks in the tension of facing different countries, different nationalities. It was a precious opportunity for each child that born and brought up in China, to observe and to experience different regional culture, to exchange and to learn in diversified multinational environment. For them, it was a completely unfamiliar and challenging life experience.

At the children's art school in Munich, little reporters showed their talents—drawing, handcraft, ceramic skills and calligraphy, and they were praised by the teachers of the children's art school in Munich. In the center of Stuttgart's

Palace Square, the little reporters introduced their hometown Chengdu to the local people in fluent English. Siegfried Houk, a 74-year-old German, praised the children for their courage and intelligence after learning the background of their trip. Just as Ms. Wang from Chengdu Radio and TV Station, leader of Marco Polo Team put it, this journey provided opportunity for students to measure the Belt and Road by their own foot, to feel the beauty of this grand area, to develop personal affectionate ties with the local people.

Education is a process that foster cognitive development. In a diversified multinational environment, "little panda reporters", dedicated to the initiative enthusiastically, felt like part of it, visited and communicated with local people friendly. Whether in the German Allianz Arena or in Strasbourg or Marseilles, whether in Florence—the birthplace of European Renaissance or in Vatican—the world's smallest country which have the world's largest church, "little panda reporters" told people of different countries lively that the Belt and Road is a road to mutual understanding, mutual appreciation, mutual respect, a road to world peace.

At the Chinese Embassy in Italy, ambassador Zhang Aishan, Director of the Information Office, met with "little panda reporters" on behalf of Ambassador Li Ruiyu. Mr. Zhang attentively and kindly listened to the experience and feelings of the students about this journey. "The panda reporters"

told Mr. Zhang that along the way, they had gained a deeper understanding of China's development and of the importance of the Silk Road in the heart of the people all over the world. While confronted with difficulties, everyone tried hard to solve problems, and they improved their mental quality, enhanced self-care ability and independent thinking ability on a daily bases. "The people-to-people bond is the most important and crucial," Mr. Zhang told them, "The 'little panda reporter' campaign has promoted exchanges between Chengdu and European countries. In each country along, you sang the Chinese folk song *Jasmine* and read the poem *Happy Rain on a Spring Night*. Your campaign had drawn great attention of the public, and your cover of the story surely brought closer contact between the people."

The ancient Silk Road once crossed continents and oceans, turned a new leaf in the history of human civilization. The revivial of Belt and Road is to put wings on China's development and promote the common prosperity of the countries along the routes. Its vision is taking root in the hearts of people all over the world, and the grand blueprint for the development of the Silk Road is spreading.

The Belt and Road initiative has brought boundless vitality and bright future to people all over the world. It is in this historical context that the "little panda reporters" have made their own efforts and contributions. Young people should be concerned about his family, his country and the world. "Everyone being responsible for the fate of his country" has been the determination of the chinese people. "Little panda reporters" should have the self−confidence and ambition of "the world rise and fall, who is the one in charge but me"! The initiative is the embodiment of the China Dream. There is a reason to believe that to move forward along the road to socialism with Chinese characteristics, we must be able to achieve the great rejuvenation of the Chinese nation, the China Dream and the dream of world peace!

"熊猫小记者"马可·波罗队2018年夏季活动照片

7月31日"熊猫小记者"夏文涛向中国驻慕尼黑总领馆教育领事黄崇岭赠送礼物

8月一日在德国慕尼黑蔚来汽车设计中心参观

▲8月2日在德国斯图加特皇宫广场做快闪介绍成都

▲8月4日在比利时安特卫普超市寻找成都制造

▲8月4日走进中国驻比利时大使馆，向中国驻比利时大使馆经商参赞郭建军和政新处主任丘建明提问

▲8月4日走进中国驻比利时大使馆，向中国驻比利时大使馆经商参赞郭建军和政新处主任丘建明提问

▲8月4日在中国驻比利时大使馆与中国驻比利时大使馆经商参赞郭建军和政新处主任丘建明合影留念

▲8月5日 "熊猫小记者"夏文涛与比利时华人青年联合会会长进行交流

▲8月5日在荷兰鹿特丹港,感受"一带一路"欧洲站终点魅力

▲8月6日走进中国驻荷兰大使馆,使馆政治处主任刘研耐心地向孩子们介绍了中荷两国在经贸、文化、教育等各个领域的合作现状

▲8月6日与中国驻荷兰大使馆工作人员合影

第三章

郑和队
新闻行动

Chapter Three
Zheng He Team

记者
球接力活动

Global Relaying ChengDu,China

郑和 (1371—1433)

　　中国明朝航海家、外交家。原姓马，名和，小名三宝，又作三保，云南昆阳(今晋宁区昆阳街道)宝山乡知代村人。1405—1433年,郑和率领2.7万人组成的庞大船队七下西洋，经东南亚、印度洋到达红海和非洲，遍访亚非30多个国家和地区，建立并巩固了海上丝绸之路，播撒了友谊的种子，促进了经济贸易发展，增进了中国与亚非各国的文化交流，为世界文明进步做出了巨大贡献。

Zheng He (1371—1433) was a Chinese navigator and diplomat in the Ming Dynasty, who was originally named Ma He, nicknamed "Three Treasure" or Sanbao. He was born in Zhidai Village, Baoshan Township, Kunyang Town (now called Kunyang Subdistrict, Jinning District), Yunnan Province. From 1405 to 1433, Zheng He led a huge fleet of more than 27000 crew members, sailed seven times to the South Seas successively. The expeditions covered the Southeast Asia, the Indian Ocean, the Red Sea and as far as Africa. They visited more than 30 countries and regions in Asia and Africa, established and consolidated the maritime silk route. Zheng He's expedition enhanced friendship and promoted the economic and trade as well as cultural exchanges between China and Asian and African countries. The voyages made great contribution to world civilization.

❝ 是祖国的强大，让汉语走进了新加坡的课堂；是"一带一路"的合作倡议，让我们有机会走进新加坡的课堂。

With the development of the motherland, Chinese language courses are offered in Singapore schools. It is the One Belt One Road initiative that offers us the opportunity to enter into Singapore's classes. **❞**

杨冯思言

9岁

成都市武侯实验小学

▲新加坡鱼尾狮公园 （摄影 刘云/视界）

一堂快乐的作文课

Oh!

▲南亚风情·新加坡·市容 （摄影 邹新华/视界）

2017年8月6日，我们一行14个小伙伴在领队蕾蕾姐姐的带领下，来到了花园城市——**新加坡**。

我们来到了新加坡社区学校，与当地的小朋友交流。社区学校主要为该社区的小朋友提供语文、数学或其他学科的教学。他们的课程都是用英语讲授的，唯独作文课用汉语讲授，我们正好赶上了一堂作文课。

走进课堂，20多个同学整齐地坐在教室里欢迎我们的到来，虽然我们互相并不认识，但一见面就被他们的热情感动了。

小贴士

　　新加坡：新加坡由64个岛屿组成，主岛新加坡岛占全国面积的90%以上。新加坡几乎没有农村，境内草茂花繁，整洁美丽，道路两旁树木成荫，街头到处是小花园、小草坪，花香草绿，空气清新，因此被世界公认为"花园城市国家"。

▲南亚风情·新加坡·市容
　（摄影 邹新华/视界）

▲快乐的作文课

我们彼此做了自我介绍，心中的陌生感慢慢消失了。上课的铃声响后，作文课老师走进教室，这是一位美丽的女老师，说一口标准的普通话，我们感到很吃惊。我们后来得知，她是新加坡的第二代华人。

这堂作文课的内容是看图写话，与我们的教学类似，同学们先看书上的图画，然后发挥想象力，用文字表达图画的意思。老师先让我们准备了10多分钟，然后让几位同学谈谈自己的写作思路。我紧张极了，生怕被老师点名。

安静的教室里突然响起了我的名字，我硬着头皮站起

来，迅速地理了一下思路，清了清嗓子，把想到的情节大声地说了出来。讲述完毕后，我看看老师，看看同行的小伙伴们，再看看新加坡的小伙伴们，他们的眼神中都充满了赞许。

▲在作文课上积极回答问题

老师向我竖起了大拇指："真棒，我为你骄傲！"同行的小伙伴们像是受到了鼓舞，纷纷举手回答问题了。当然，新加坡的同学也不甘落后，就这样，本来紧张的课堂一下子活跃起来了。作文老师点评完同学们的回答后，开始有声有色地讲起了这幅图，她时而眨眨眼，时而皱皱眉，时而声音低沉，时而开怀大笑。她的讲述令我们印象深刻。

　　课堂时间不多了，老师总结性地讲道："感谢远道而来的中国同学，是你们让我参与了一次难忘而又快乐的课堂交流，欢迎你们下次再来。"这时教室里响起了热烈的掌声。

　　下课的铃声响起，我们这次的社区课堂交流也要结束了。我们和当地的同学们互赠了礼物和卡片，郑重地邀请他们到中国学习，感受我们中国的课堂。通过与新加坡小朋友共同上课，我们进一步增加了彼此的了解。

　　排队走出教室时，我看到同行的小伙伴们脸上都挂着笑容，我知道每个人都和我一样的快乐。

　　我的心情也久久不能平静。是祖国的强大，让汉语走进了新加坡的课堂；是"一带一路"的合作倡议，让我们有机会走进新加坡的课堂，认识更多的朋友。

A Happy Composition Class

Yang Fengsiyan（9 years old, Chengdu Wuhou Experimental Primary School）

On August 6, 2017, a group of 14 kids led by Leilei, arrived in the garden city, Singapore.

We arrived at a Singapore community school to communicate with the local children. The school provides language, mathematics and other subjects for children in this community. All of the courses are taught in English except the composition course, which is taught in Chinese. We were just in time for a composition course.

As we walked into the classroom, more than two dozen students sat in the classroom in good order and greeted us warmly. Although we didn't know each other, we were touched by their enthusiasm. We introduced ourselves to each other, and gradually we got familiar with each other. When the bell rang, the teacher came into the classroom. She was a beautiful lady who spoke standard Mandarin. We were surprised. We later learned that she was the second generation Chinese in

171

Singapore.

Similar to our Chinese teaching method, in this composition course, the students first were asked to watch some pictures, then used their imagination to try to describe the pictures. The teacher gave us more than ten minutes to prepare for the discussion, then she named some students to talk about their thoughts. I was very nervous about being named by the teacher.

In the quiet classroom, suddenly my name was mentioned. I had to stand up. I quickly cleared my mind and throat, and told the story out loudly. When I finished, I looked at the teacher, my peers and my new friends in Singapore. In their eyes I saw approval.

The teacher gave me a thumbs up: "Great! I'm proud of you!" My partners seemed to be encouraged, and they raised their hands to answer questions. Of course, the Singapore students did not want to be left behind, thus the silence was broken in the classroom. After the teacher commented on the students' answers, she began to tell the story about the picture lively. While telling the story, she sometimes blinked and frowned, sometimes in a low voice, and sometimes laugh out loudly. We were impressed by her story.

The class was almost over. The teacher said, "Thank you, all the Chinese students. It is you who make this class happy and unforgettable. Welcome to come again." Warm applause

resonated in the classroom.

The bell rang, and our community class was over. We exchanged gifts and cards with our Singapore classmates and invited them to come to China to join in our Chinese class. By sharing lessons with the children of Singapore, we had further increased our understanding of each other.

As I walked out of the classroom, I saw smiles on everyone's face, and I knew everyone was as happy as I was.

At the same time, I feel excited. With the development of the motherland, Chinese language courses are offered in Singapore schools. It is the Belt and Road initiative that offers us the opportunity to enter into the classes in Singapore and meet more friends.

" 随着中国的强大，随着"一带一路"合作的推进，将会有更多的中国元素融入马来西亚，祖国正以它博大的胸怀走向世界。

With China's development and the promotion of the Belt and Road initiative, more and more Chinese elements will be melted into Malaysian culture. Our motherland is opening up to the world. "

成佩玲

10岁

成都市锦官新城小学

马来西亚乐高乐园的中国元素

2017年暑假，我们队沿着伟大航海家郑和的足迹，去了新加坡和马来西亚，我印象最深的是马来西亚的乐高乐园。

2017年8月8日，我和小伙伴们走进了马来西亚的乐高乐园。一进大门，我就被眼前的景象吸引住了，巨大的乐高玩具威武雄壮地耸立着，我情不自禁地用手摸了摸。它们可是用一块块的乐高积木拼接起来的，这得费多少工夫啊！简单的积木却拼出了如此多的情境，这也许正是乐

▲ 在乐高乐园留影

高乐园独特的魅力吧。

我正在感叹时，一个熟悉的场景映入眼帘，那不是我们中国的**万里长城**吗！马来西亚的乐高乐园里怎么会有中国的长城呢？看着用乐高积木堆拼而成的"长城"，我们好奇地向老师请教。

万里长城：中国古代为防御游牧民族南下而修建的军事防御工程，是一道高大、坚固而连绵不断的长垣，用以阻隔敌骑的行动。长城不是一道单纯孤立的城墙，而是以城墙为主体，同大量的城、障、亭、标相结合的防御体系。

原来，乐高乐园用积木别出心裁地原样"复制"了一段中国的万里长城。

在乐高乐园，我们不仅玩了惊险刺激的过山车，

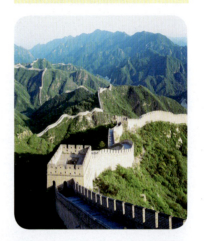

▲在乐高乐园

还坐上超级摩天轮到令人毛骨悚然的古堡探险。不同肤色的游客都迈着轻盈的步伐，激动地交流着自己的感受。这不正是我们宣传成都的机会吗？我们可是"熊猫小记者"啊！

于是，我们向游人宣讲，成都有大熊猫、青城山、都江堰、杜甫草堂、武侯祠、宽窄巷子、东郊记忆……还有名扬天下的川菜。

我大方地走到一位外国阿姨面前，礼貌地用英语说道："Excuse me, we are 'little panda reporters' from China...Thank you very much！"那位外国阿姨竖起大拇指，微笑着对我说："Oh，very good！"

不知不觉，我们在乐高乐园度过了愉快的一天。离开时，我想，随着"一带一路"合作的推进，将会有更多的中国元素融入马来西亚，祖国正以她博大的胸怀走向世界。

Chinese Elements in Legoland in Malaysia

Cheng Peiling（10 years old, Chengdu Jinguan New City Primary School）

In the summer of 2017, our team followed the footsteps of Zheng He the great navigator, went to Singapore and Malaysia, and I was most impressed by Legoland in Malaysia.

On August 8, 2017, we walked into the Legoland in Malaysia. As soon as I entered the gate, I was attracted by the sight. The huge Lego buildings stood majestically, and I could not help touching them with my hands. They are made of pieces of Lego blocks. How much time it would take to set up the buildings! Such a simple building block, and yet such a marvelous scene when the blocks are pieced together, which may be the unique charm of Lego.

As I was exclaiming, a familiar scene came into view. Wasn't that the Great Wall of China？Why was the Great Wall in Malaysia's Legoland? Looking at the Great Wall made of Lego blocks, we asked our teacher. It turned out that the designers

had "copied" a part of the Great Wall with Lego blocks.

At Legoland, we not only had a thrilling ride on the roller coaster, but also sat on a super Ferris wheel to explore the creepy old castle. There were so many people in the park. The tourists with different skin colors were walking with light steps and excitedly communicating their feelings. Wasn't that our chance to promote Chengdu? This was one of the main purposes of our trip. Therefore, we told the tourists that in Chengdu, there were giant pandas, Mount Qingcheng, Dujiangyan Irrigation System, Du fu's Thatched Cottage, Wuhou Shrine, the Narrow and Wide Alleys, the Memorial Park of the Eastern Suburbs...Not to mention the famous Sichuan cuisine.

I went toward a foreign lady and said politely in English, "Excuse me, we are 'little panda reporters' from China...Thank you very much! "The lady gave me a thumb-up and said, "Oh, very good!"

Before we realized, it's time to go. We had a good day at Legoland. Upon leaving, I thought, with the development of China, along with the advancement of the Belt and Road cooperation, there will be more Chinese elements melt into Malaysian culture, our motherland is opening up to the world.

追寻郑和的足迹，做一名传播中华文明的使者。

I wish to follow Zheng He's example and become a messenger of Chinese civilization.

潘希睿

9岁

成都市武侯实验小学

在马来西亚
寻找郑和的足迹

2017年8月，我举着"郑和队"的队旗，到了新加坡和马来西亚。

▲寻找郑和的足迹

临行前，爸爸妈妈给我讲了郑和的事迹，我知道郑和是云南人，因为带领船队七下西洋而被世人传颂。因此，我特别期待行程中的马六甲。

▲寻找郑和的足迹

▲马六甲红屋 （摄影 刘云/视界）

小贴士

马六甲：马来西亚的一个州，首府马六甲市，别称麻六甲，位于马来西亚半岛南部，濒临马六甲海峡。它是曾经的马六甲王国所在地，郑和下西洋曾有六次在此停靠，如今是马六甲海峡这条海上生命线的咽喉所在。

2017年8月9日，我们来到**马六甲**，先后参观了郑和博物馆、三宝井、三宝寺、温古堂等。

郑和博物馆位于马六甲河北岸圣保罗山上，是一幢红色的三层建筑。走进馆里，中国的宫灯装饰和郑和的塑像映入我的眼帘。那些宝船与实物，让我感到行前了解的郑和仿佛活了过来。那大幅的郑和航海图告诉了我们郑和七下西洋的路线，以及船员们的生活场景和他们应对海上各种风浪时的情形。一件件文物，带着我们跟随郑和的脚步去感受沿途各国的风土人情，了解他们当时带去的中华文明。

在航海技术展区，我们见识了明朝高超的船舶制造技术，了解到郑和的船队是如何在海上识别方向的。让我印象最深的是模拟郑和舰队开航的"海上飞燕阵"模型而制作的160多艘船模。船上有炮台、帆、缆绳、舷窗，还有很多我叫不出名字的工具，做得非常逼真。船只大小不同，浩浩荡荡排列着，像一只只飞燕，非常壮观。这是中国曾经强盛的明证，而今，"一带一路"倡议必将有助于中华民族的伟大复兴。

走出郑和馆，我们参观了附近的三宝

井。传说这些井是郑和在马六甲时凿下的，现在看来虽然只是井口加上了盖板的井，但当年此井中水却被马六甲人民称作"神

水",饮用或者冲凉都可以延年益寿,所以每天在井边打水的人络绎不绝,取水解渴,取水许愿……这也是中华文化福泽当地的明证。马六甲人民也没有忘记郑和,通过三宝井和郑和博物馆来纪念他。

我们得知当地的学校把郑和的故事写进了历史教科书。再想到我们这支"熊猫小记者"队叫"郑和队",便不觉想起 "熊猫小记者"的誓词:"我将秉承丝路精神,践行和平理念,寻访万里疆海,加强与外国小朋友之间的沟通交流,增进中外友谊,弘扬中国文明,展现成都风采……"

Seeking for Zheng He's Footprint in Malaysia

Pan Xirui（9 years old, Chengdu Wuhou Experimental Primary School）

In August 2017, as a member of Zheng He Team, I arrived in Singapore and Malaysia.

Upon leaving, my parents told me the life story of Zheng He. I knew he was from Yunnan Province, and he was known for his voyages to the Western Seas. Therefore, among all the stops in the itinerary, I especially looked forward to Malacca.

On August 9, 2017, we came to Malacca, and visited Zheng He Museum, Sanbao(Zheng He's nickname) Well, Sanbao Temple, Wen Gutang Hakka Hall and so on.

Located on Saint Paulo Hill to the north of Malacca River, the museum is a red three-floor building. In the hall, statues of Zheng He and many Chinese palace lanterns can be seen. The treasure ship and relics reminded me of the hero Zheng He who I got to know before the trip. The large charts showed us the route of Zheng He's voyages to the Western Seas, as well as the life scenes of the crew and various responses to storms at sea. The cultural relics demonstrated the customs of the countries along Zheng He's sea route, brought us back to the prosperous Chinese civilization at that time.

In the navigation technology exhibition area, we saw the superb shipbuilding technology of the Ming Dynasty, and learned how Zheng He's fleet was oriented. What impressed me most was 160 odd ship models simulating those of Zheng He's fleet. There were batteries, sails, cables and porthole, and a lot of tools that I could not name. The boats were of different sizes, and they were arranged like a flying swallow. This is an evidence of the strength of China's past. This is a sign that now the Belt and Road initiative surely rejuvenates the Chinese nation.

Out of Zheng He Museum, we visited the nearby Sanbao Well. In the legend these wells were dug when Zheng He was in Malacca, now they were covered with a well cover. The water from the well was called "Divine Water" by the Malacca people. They thought drinking the water or bathing with the water could lengthen lives. So everyday people draw water from the well to drink or make wishes at the edge of the well...The well is also a token of Chinese culture. The people of Malacca did not forget Zheng He, they memorized him through the Sanbao Well and Zheng He Museum.

We learned from local school that the Malaysian people had written the story of Zheng He into the history textbooks. Since our team is named after Zheng He, it reminded me of our oath: "I will be adhering to the spirit of the Silk Road, practice concept of peace cross the sea, try my best to strengthen the communication with foreign children, enhance the friendship between China and foreign countries and spread China's culture, show the world the charm of Chengdu..."

> 温古堂让我了解了先辈们创业的艰辛，以及他们对马来西亚文化的贡献。

At Wengutang, I learned about how hard our ancestors set up their business and their contributions to Malaysian culture.

龚玥

10岁

成都市锦江区教师进修校附属小学

温古堂见闻

▲温古堂留影

2017年8月9日，我们"熊猫小记者"郑和队一行10多人参观了马六甲的温古堂。温古堂是2014年**客家人**筹办的"传说古城"故事馆，其目的是让民众重温古时候的点点滴滴。里面展出了先辈南来靠岸登陆后，从事各种行业筚路蓝缕的痕迹，让参观者随着墙上的画面和展品，了解当年的情景，记住那段历史。

小贴士

客家人：自秦朝至今在南方地区居住的有两千多年历史的一个重要群体，是广东本地的主要族群之一，也是江西和福建本地的重要族群之一。

据会馆中文献记载，1882年至1910年，每年来马来西亚的客家人有数十万。客家人勤劳、聪明，很快在异国他乡站稳脚跟，渐渐融入当地各行各业，遍地开花。客家人为马来西亚的社会经济发展做出了重大贡献，比如采矿、种植、印刷、珠宝等众多领域都有客家人的创业史迹；

同时在普及华文教育、传播中华文化等方面，客家人也功不可没。

马六甲是很多广东客家人踏上异国他乡的首站，这里留下了不少客家人的历史印迹。温古堂通过实物展示和画面解说，让我们了解当年先辈劳动的场面，如打铁、打金、做鞋、酿造酱油等。同时，温古堂还记载了各行各业的故事以及先辈们留下的痕迹。店铺的装饰风

▲在温古堂认真听讲解

格大都保留着百年前的模样，且都有中文招牌。这些辛苦劳作的场面我是第一次看到，它让我了解到先辈们在异国他乡生活的艰苦。

而今，客家人积极组织当地青年到中国，增进中国与马来西亚的民间交流。随着"一带一路"倡议的深入推进，马来西亚与中国的经济交流不断增强，这也推动了马来西亚与中国的共同发展。

▲参观温古堂

At Wengutang

Gong Yue (10 years old, Affiliated Primary School of Chengdu Jinjiang District Teacher Training School)

On August 9, 2017, Zheng He Team—a group of ten odd "little panda reporters" visited Wengutang in Malacca. In 2014, Hakka community set up Wengutang—a museum about "the ancient city according to legend story". Its purpose is to bring people back to ancient times when their ancestors landed on the shore and engaged in all kinds of industries, help visitors understand the situation and remember the history through the picture illustration and exhibits.

According to literature in the hall, from 1882 to 1910, hundreds of thousands of Hakka people came to Malaysia each year. They were industrious and intelligent, soon settled down and gradually merged into foreign society. They had made great contribution to the social and economic development of Malaysia. They started business in a wide variety of industries, such as mining, planting, printing, jewelry and many other fields. At the same time, the Hakkas also contributed to

popularizing the Chinese education and spreading Chinese culture.

Malacca is the first destination of many Hakka families when they migrated to the South Asia, therefore a lot of Hakka history lies here. Through antic display and picture illustration, we caught a glimpse of labor scenes of the previous generation, such as ironing, blacksmithing, making shoes, brewing soy sauce and so on. At the same time, the stories of all walks of life of the ancestors were also leaving a trace here. Most of the shop's decorative style remained the original looking a hundred years ago, and all had Chinese signs. It was the first time I had seen these laborious scenes, and it taught me the hardship of life in a foreign country.

Today, Malaysia Hakka community actively organize local youth to experience China and promote the non-governmental exchanges between China and Malaysia. With the deepening of the Belt and Road initiative, the economic exchanges between Malaysia and China have been increasing, which has also contributed to the common development of Malaysia and China.

中国美食是世界饮食文化中一颗璀璨的明珠，愿它惠及世界。

Chinese food is a bright pearl on the crown of world cuisine. May it benefit people all over the world.

黄子函

12岁

成都市七中育才学校学道分校

漂洋过海的中国美食

2017年8月6日至8月11日，我作为"熊猫小记者"，参加了郑和队新闻行动，令我无法忘怀的是新加坡和马来西亚的美食，它们色香味俱全，让人垂涎三尺。

我回想起在两国饭店看到的菜名：番茄炒蛋、炒空心菜、清蒸鱼……怎么会有我们中国的菜肴呢？我上网一查，知道了两国的菜肴都与中国美食有关系。

▲中国美食

▲中国美食地图

▲Bak Kut Teh 肉骨茶

　　在新加坡的中式美食中，粤菜十分受欢迎，它以清淡出名。在新加坡饭店里可以见到北京的烤鸭、上海的鳝鱼、潮州的卤鸭、客家酿豆腐、辛辣的川菜等中国菜肴。在马来西亚，也有很多中国的特色菜，如酿豆腐、海南鸡饭、香港点心等。新加坡与马来西亚人民将中国菜与它们本土的菜融为一体，让菜肴变得更加琳琅满目！

　　这次行动中，我们一方面介绍成都和中国的文化，另一方面也要去探查新加坡和马来西亚当地的文化。在马来西亚，我品尝了当地的特色菜：**肉骨茶**。此"茶"非彼"茶"，是一道家喻户晓的排骨药材汤，没有鲜艳的色泽，只有扑鼻的清香，鲜美之中又带着药材的味道。在新加坡，我品尝了海南鸡饭。海南鸡饭是将白切鸡和饭融在一起，白糯的米饭配上酸甜可口、肉劲十足的白切鸡，使中国菜也变得更独特、更美味了。

小贴士

肉骨茶：一道猪肉药材汤，汤料完全没有茶叶的成分，而是以猪肉和猪骨，混合中药及香料，熬煮数小时的浓汤。"肉骨"采用的是猪的肋排(俗称排骨)，而"茶"则是一道排骨药材汤。20世纪初，此道菜由马来西亚福建籍华侨首创，其后盛行于东南亚一带。

为什么新加坡每个饭店里都会有中国的传统美食呢？这是因为新加坡有将近280万的华人，占新加坡总人口的74.1%。渐渐地，新加坡每个饭店里都有了华人爱吃的中国菜！并且，新加坡菜和马来西亚菜也将中国菜和本地菜混合在一起，形成了一种独特的风格。

通过这次活动，我从新加坡和马来西亚两国的中国美食中，感受到中国与两国深厚的友谊。

▲Laksa 叻沙

▲Chilli Crab 辣椒蟹

Chinese Delicacies across the Sea

Huang Zihan（12 years old, Chengdu No.7 Yucai Middle School, Xuedao Campus）

From August 6, to August 11, 2017, as a "little panda reporter", I participated in the activity of News Relaying by Zheng He Team. I couldn't forget the delicious food of Singapore and Malaysia.

I recalled dishes on the menu I saw in the two hotels: scrambled eggs with tomato, fried swamp cabbage, steamed fish...How did the Chinese dishes appear on the menus in restaurants of Singapore and Malaysia? I googled online and found out that the dishes in both countries are related to Chinese cuisine.

In Singapore, Cantonese cuisine is very popular and is known for its light flavor. We had seen Beijing roast duck, Shanghai cooked eel, Chaozhou braised duck, Hakka toufu, spicy Sichuan cuisine and other Chinese dishes. In Malaysia, there are also many Chinese special cooking, such as

stuffed bean curd, Hainan chicken rice and Hong Kong snacks. People in Singapore and Malaysia blend Chinese food with their local dishes to create a new diversified style of cooking!

During this trip, we introduced the culture of Chengdu and China; on the other hand, we explored the local culture of Singapore and Malaysia. In Malaysia, I tasted local specialties: bak kut teh. This so-called "tea" is not the real tea, it is a kind of well-known pork ribs and herb soup. It looks plain, yet smells good with herbal flavor. It is delicious. In Singapore, I also tasted Hainan chicken rice. Hainan chicken rice is a blend of boiled sliced chicken and rice. The glutinous rice matches well with the boiled sliced chicken with sweet and sour flavor. Chinese food hence tastes more unique and delicious.

Why does Chinese traditional food can be found in nearly every restaurant in Singapore? That's because there are nearly 2.8 million Chinese in Singapore, with the proportion of 74.1% of the whole population. Gradually, there are Chinese food in every restaurant in Singapore! Also, Singapore and Malaysian cuisine blends Chinese and local dishes and develop into a unique style.

Through this trip, I experienced affectionate tie between China, Singapore and Malaysia from the Chinese cuisine in the two countries.

> **"** 中国公学是中华文明的传播者，愿中华文明惠及东南亚人民。

Sekolah Jenis Kebangsaan (China) is a spreader of Chinese culture. May Chinese culture benefit the people of southeast Asia. **"**

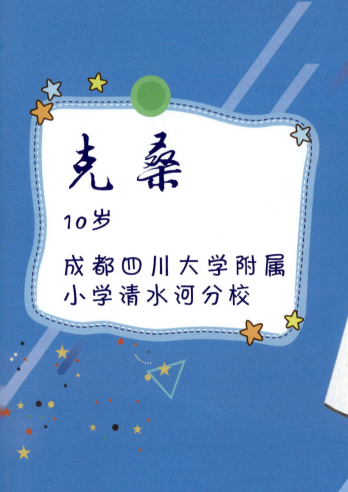

克桑

10岁

成都四川大学附属
小学清水河分校

孩子们的跨国友谊

▲马来西亚·马六甲 （摄影 邬新华/视界）　　▲马六甲红屋 （摄影 刘云/视界）

　　600多年前，明朝的航海家郑和率领庞大的船队七下西洋，这是中国历史上空前的历时28年、涉及亚非37个国家和地区的伟大航行，使明代中国在海外贸易、对外影响上都达到了前所未有的高度。

▲南亚风情·马来西亚·马六甲 （摄影 邬新华/视界）

　　2017年8月10日，我们来到了郑和下西洋时在马来西亚六次停靠的地点——马六甲。马六甲是一个美丽的海滨城市。一路上，我们看到的都是整洁的村庄街道、绿油油的植物与灌木丛等异国风光，突然，一所名字与中国息息相关的学校——中国公学出现在了眼前。在干净整洁的校门口，我们受到了中国公学的老师与同学们的热情欢迎。

▲参观中国公学

走进学校礼堂，我们与马六甲小朋友们的交流在一片欢声笑语中开始了。中国公学的校长与我们热情握手，向我们赠送小礼物——具有马六甲民族服饰特色的冰箱贴和温古堂明信片。我们做了自我介绍，马六甲的小朋友们也用流利的中文做了自我介绍。在交流中，我向马六甲的小朋友们介绍了我们家乡美丽的**九寨沟**。

▲九寨沟五花海秋景　摄影　王达军

我们与中国公学的小朋友们玩起了马来西亚的传统游戏：放珠子。在一个木盘里，有10个小格、2个大格，两队人轮流往格子

小贴士

九寨沟：位于四川省阿坝藏族羌族自治州九寨沟县境内，是中国第一个以保护自然风景为主要目的的自然保护区，因沟内有树正寨、荷叶寨、则查洼寨等九个藏族村寨坐落在这片高山湖泊群中而得名。

里放珠子，最后哪一队放的珠子多哪一队就获胜。我们分成5组一起玩这个游戏。我们有不会或不懂的地方，中国公学的同学们都会耐心地教我们，让我们感觉既轻松又愉快。随后，我们又玩起了跳房子，

▲与中国公学的小朋友玩游戏

尽管有的同学跳得很笨拙，但大家都没有一点儿埋怨之意，我们都很珍惜彼此的友谊。

我们还参观了学校的教学楼。虽然他们的教学设施、教学环境没有我们成都学校的好，但看着他们学习是那样认真，对我们是那样热情，我很受鼓舞。

快乐的时光总是过得很快。我们依依不舍地离开了中国公学，但我们与中国公学小朋友的友谊却不会中断。这短暂的一天给我留下了许多美好的回忆，在未来的日子里，我与马来西亚小朋友们的友谊会越来越深。

▲参观中国公学

Transnational Friendship among Children

Ke Sang（10 years old, Affiliated Primary School of Sichuan University, Qingshuihe Campus）

More than 600 years ago, in Ming Dynasty, navigator Zheng He led a huge fleet and expedited to the south seas for seven times successively. The expeditions involving 37 countries and regions in Asia and Africa lasted for 28 years, which was unprecedented in the history of China. Through this voyage the external trade and influence of China reaching to unprecedented heights.

On August 10, 2017, we arrived at the site where Zheng He stopped for six times in his seven expeditions to Malaysia—Malacca. Malacca is a beautiful coastal city. Along the way, clean and tidy village streets, green plants and bushes and other exotic scenery greeted our eyes. All of a sudden, a name closely related to China—Chinese Public School(Sekolah Jenis Kebangsaan)—was coming into sight. At the clean and tidy school gate, we were warmly welcomed by teachers and students.

From the very beginning, the school hall was full of happy and cheerful conversation and laughter of the children. The headmaster of Sekolah

Jenis Kebangsaan shook hands with us warmly and gave us small gifts—refrigerator stickers with Malacca costumes on them and postcards about Wengutang. Then, we introduced ourselves, and the children of Malacca introduced themselves in fluent Chinese. In the communication, I introduced the beautiful Jiuzhaigou Valley in our hometown to them.

Next, we played a traditional Malaysian game with each other: beads. In a wooden tray, there were 10 small squares and two large squares, and the two teams took turns to put beads into the square, and the team which put more beads into the square would win the game. We split up into five groups to play the game. When we did not understand or did not know how to act, they would patiently teach us, and made us feel relaxed and happy. After that, we played the jump house. Although some students jumped awkwardly, but nobody complained. We all valued our friendship.

Finally, we visited the school building. Although their teaching facilities and teaching environment were not as good as those of our schools, it was very encouraging to watch them study hard. They were so enthusiastic.

Happy time always passes quickly. Although we left reluctantly, our friendship with the students in Chinese Public School would not be separated. This short day left many good memories for me. In the future, my friendship with Malaysia kids will be deeper and deeper.

66 愿中马两国人民的友谊万古常青。

May the friendship between China and Malaysia be everlasting. **99**

卢昱霏

10岁

成都市泡桐树小学

▲中马铁路开工建设了

中马铁路筑牢两国友谊

我们在马来西亚虽然只待了几天，但马来西亚却给我留下了深刻的印象。在马来西亚，我看到很多中国元素，感受到中、马两国之间的紧密联系。当我听到中马铁路正在建设时，激动的心情难以言表。

中马铁路建设长度约600公里，预计在2022年完工。项目规划起点为吉隆坡北部的鹅唛，终点为吉兰丹州的瓦卡巴鲁。此线路跨越马来半岛4个州，连接东海岸各州首府、重要城镇和关丹港、甘马挽港等，沿线有400多万居民，建成后将成为贯通马来半岛东西方向的铁路运输干线和经济动脉，从而结束马来西亚东海岸部分地方没有铁路连接的历史。

马来西亚地理位置优越，扼守马六甲海峡，是海上丝绸之路的重要节点。中、马合作建设的马来西亚东海岸铁路项目正式开工，不仅推进了中国 "一带一路"倡议在东南亚的重要实践，也将给马来西亚带来可观的经济增长，甚至撬动整个东南亚经济的发展。

▲中央电视台新闻频道报道中马铁路

中马铁路建成，还将促进东盟互联互通。它是中国"一带一路"倡议中最突出的项目之一，旨在打造现代化的"丝绸之路"，将世界第二大经济体通过陆路走廊连接到东南亚。中马铁路是我国"一带一路"倡议的一个重要组成部分，建成后将会给两国的铁路建设带来新的发展机遇，必将造福于两国人民。而中马铁路的优质合作，不仅为我国实现中国铁路"走出去"的战略目标做出重要贡献，更将进一步推动中国和东南亚国家的交流合作。

中国和马来西亚的友谊历史悠久。在北宋时期，马来西亚就与中国有着各种各样的经贸往来。明朝的航海家郑和七次下西洋时，在马来西

▲吉隆坡双子星塔 （摄影 刘云/视界）

亚有长时间的停留。由于交往密切，马来西亚与中国有着相似的文化。到了近现代，许许多多的华人下南洋，定居马来西亚，马来西亚与中国的联系更加紧密了。在马来西亚，30％以上的居民是华人，90％以上的居民有华人血统。如今，中马铁路的开工，将使两国人民的友谊更加深厚。

Long Last Friendship between China and Malaysia

Lu Yufei（10 years old，Chengdu Paotongshu Primary School）

In a short stay of a few days in Malaysia, I was deeply impressed by Malaysia. In Malaysia, I saw a lot of Chinese imprints and felt the close ties between China and Malaysia. When I heard the news that China-Malaysia railway was under construction, my excitement was beyond words.

The railway is about 600 kilometers long and is expected to be completed by 2022. The project is planned to start at Gombak in northern Kuala Lumpur, and the destination is Vakabalu, in Kelantan State. The line runs across four states on Malay Peninsula, connecting state capitals, important towns of the east coast and major ports such as Kemaman Port, with more than 400 residents along the way. After construction, it will become east-west railway transport trunk lines and economic artery in the Malay Peninsula, putting an end to the history that parts of Malaysia's east coast have no railway.

Malaysia enjoys important geological location on the maritime Silk Road, guarding the strategic point of the Strait of Malacca. China-Malaysia

cooperation of construction the railway project officially starts in Malaysia's east coast. This will not only promote the Belt and Road initiative to practice in southeast Asia, but also bring considerable economic growth to Malaysia, even drive the economic development of southeast Asia.

The completion of China–Malaysia railway will also promote ASEAN communication. It is one of the most prominent projects in the Belt and Road initiative, which aims to build a modern Silk Road that connects the world's second largest economy to southeast Asia through land corridors. China–Malaysia railway is an important part of the Belt and Road development, which will bring new development opportunities to the railway construction of the two countries and will benefit people of the two countries. The quality cooperation between China and Malaysia railway will not only make an important contribution to China's strategic goal of "going global", but also further promote exchanges and cooperation between China and southeast Asian countries.

China and Malaysia have a long history of friendship. During the Northern Song Dynasty, Malaysia had various economic and trade relations with China. Zheng He, the navigator of the Ming Dynasty, had a long stay in Malaysia during his seven voyages to the south seas. Malaysia has a similar culture with China due to its close bond with China. In modern times, a large number of Chinese people had settled in Malaysia, which brought Malaysia closer to China. In Malaysia, more than 30% of the population is Chinese, and more than 90% are of Chinese ancestry. Today, with the construction of the railway, the friendship between the two countries will last long.

" 我希望将来成为一名大使，为中外友好贡献自己的力量。

I hope to become an ambassador in the future and contribute to the friendship between China and foreign countries. **"**

程璐

8岁

成都市锦江外国语小学

"熊猫小记者"游学记

2017年8月6日，我们坐着大巴车，来到了新加坡的胡姬花园。一下车，映入我眼帘的是一片花的海洋，芳香扑鼻而来，我仿佛变成了一只翩翩起舞的蝴蝶……在这里，我认识了卓锦万代兰，听说它是新加坡的国花，我不禁想起了成都的市花——芙蓉花。

告别胡姬花园，我们来到了新加坡一所社区学校。在这所学校，我们交了很多好朋友，还与他们一起上了作文课。课堂上，大家都聚精会神地听讲，积极举手回答问题。课后，老师还给我们布置了作文作业。真是有趣的一堂课！在课余时间，我们与新加坡小朋友一起玩游戏，一起为熊猫涂色。最终，我们把熊猫涂成了粉色，逗得大家哈哈大笑……分别

▲快乐的作文课

时，听说新加坡小朋友不久就要到成都体验我们的课程，我好期待这一天的到来。

最让我高兴的是参观马来西亚乐高乐园。它是亚洲第一座乐高主题公园，里面的建筑全部是由乐高积木搭成的，精心的设计、巧妙的搭建，像极了曾经在我梦里出现了很多次的殿堂……我们在这里欢声笑语，尽情玩耍，拼凑自己的梦想，我多么希望时间能暂停呀。

我们一路旅行、

一路学习，我们还参观了马来西亚郑和博物馆、温古堂、粉红清真寺、马六甲、荷兰红屋……在郑和博物馆，老师给我们讲了当年郑和船队如何帮助当地群众的故事；在温古堂，我们向馆长赠送了代表成都的蜀绣，并介绍了成都的文化，得到馆长的好评和赞扬。在中国驻马来西亚大使馆，张叔叔耐心地接受了我们的采访。他希望我们回国后好好学习，多和马来西亚的小朋友交流、学习。

　　此次活动，我们做了很多有意义的事：在街头向陌生人介绍成都，以及记录他们对成都的了解。在街头，我与几位华人叔叔阿姨进行了愉快的聊天。我用普通话介绍了我自己，介绍了我的学校，介绍了我的家乡成都……他们都很友好，当他们得知我才8岁时，不禁竖起大拇指，我感到骄傲与自豪。

　　这次游学，我是第一次出国，第一次离开爸爸妈妈，第一次收获那么多的外国文化，也是第一次交外国朋友，我为自己是中国人、是成都人而骄傲！

Study Tour of a "Little Panda Reporter"

Cheng Lu（8 years old, Affiliated Primary School of Chengdu Jinjiang Foreign Language Institute）

On August 6, 2017, we took a van to the Orchid Garden in Singapore. When I got out of the van, I was greeted by a sea of fragrant flowers, and I became a flying butterfly...Here, I got to know Vanda Miss Joaquim, the national flower of Singapore, which reminded me of Chengdu city flower—hibiscus flower.

Farewell to the Orchid Garden, we came to a Singapore community school. In the school, we made a lot of good friends and had a composition class with them. In class, everyone listened attentively and raised their hands to answer questions actively. After the class, the teacher gave us a composition assignment. What an interesting class! In our spare time, we played games with Singapore kids and we painted the panda doll together. Finally, we painted the panda doll in pink and everyone laughed out loudly...At the same time, I heard that the children of Singapore may come to Chengdu to experience our courses. I was looking forward to meeting them in Chengdu.

The most joyful thing for me was to visit Legoland in Malaysia. It is the first Lego theme park in Asia. Inside the park, the buildings were all made of Lego blocks with elaborate design and skillful construction, much like the palace once appeared many times in my dreams...We laughed, played, made up our dreams, and at that moment I wished time would stop.

We traveled all the way while studied all the way. We also visited the Malaysian Zheng He Museum, Wengutang, the Pink Mosque, Malacca, the Red House of the Netherlands...At Zheng He Museum, the teacher explained how Zheng He's fleet assisted the local people. In Wengutang, we presented the curator Shu embroidery of Chengdu style and introduced the culture of Chengdu. We were praised by the curator. At the Chinese embassy in Malaysia, Mr. Zhang patiently accepted our interview. He wanted us to study hard after we went back to China, and to communicate and learn from children in Malaysia.

In this journey, We did a lot of meaningful things: road show to strangers to help them understand Chengdu better. On the street, I had a pleasant chat with a few local Chinese. I introduced myself in Mandarin, introduced my school and my hometown Chengdu...They were all friendly to me, and when they learned that I was only 8 years old, they gave me a thumbs-up, and I was proud.

It was the first time I went abroad. For the first time I left my mom and dad to experience foreign culture and made foreign friends. I am proud of being a Chinese, a Chengdu child!

66 我希望自己将来像郑和一样，做一名中华文化的传播者。**99**

I hope that I will follow Zheng He's example and spread Chinese culture.

严子涵

9岁

成都师范学校附属小学

马六甲的中国印记

2017年8月，我有幸成为一名"熊猫小记者"，参加成都市广播电视台举办的全球追访"一带一路"大型公益新闻接力行动。9日，我来到马六甲这个港口城市。

在马六甲老城区的一片密集老宅区里的一条老巷子中间，有一栋建筑特别显眼，四角向上翻翘的屋顶、灰色的外墙、朱红的立柱，它那深棕色的牌匾上嵌着五个烫金大字"郑和博物馆"。博物馆既宽阔又明亮，中式木家具加现代化展柜，使人仿佛置身成都洛带的广东会馆。

▲马六甲荷兰红屋 （摄影 刘云/视界）

郑和在1405年至1433年七下西洋。其中，规模最大的一次下西洋，

▲马六甲保山庙 （摄影 刘云/视界）

郑和带着280条船、28700多人，是当时世界上规模最大的船队，船上还有饲养场、菜地等。船队多次在马六甲停留补充给养。

郑和下西洋，主要是为了传播中华文化和传统。郑和来到马六甲时，马六甲只是一个小渔村。郑和向马来人赠送了中国的瓷器、丝绸、茶叶等，并用中国特产交换当地的香料、珠宝、珊瑚等。郑和还教当地人怎样做买卖，怎么在海上划船用渔网捕鱼。

郑和对马六甲的贡献，当地人并没有忘记。在郑和博物馆里，还陈列着郑和与马来西亚皇帝交流、郑和船队的大型塑像，以及郑和带来的青花瓷、药材等。院内，至今还保留着当时郑和的专用水井。博物馆附近的一座小山，也被当地人命名为"三宝山"，纪念郑和把文明带到这

▲在温古堂认真听讲解

里。

我们来到山中的三宝寺，那典型的中式古典风格，红瓦墙、点蜡烛、用井水，无不体现着中华文化的印记。在寺中，供奉着刚毅威武的郑和立式塑像。寺内还保留着郑和下

▲马六甲保山庙 　（摄影　刘云/视界）

西洋时修建的七口井中的两口。听导游老师讲，当年郑和船上的人主要是喝雨水，但光雨水不够，所以便掘了井。井掘好后，部分井水用于船上的人员喝，部分井水给当地人喝。

在马六甲，还有一个叫"温古堂"的地方，保存着很多郑和之后，中国人来马六甲和当地人融合的遗迹。进入温古堂，里面陈列了许多马来人和中国人几百年前使用过的东西。一只只有20多厘米高的小木桶吸引了我，这么小的木桶装水也太少了吧？原来这只小木桶不是装水的，是马来人把钱装在桶里面，用绳子悬挂在屋梁上，免得被小孩乱拿。有一组照片，让我觉得特别眼熟，是中国人过春节时用的灯笼、彩带等。原来，马六甲也过春节，也把彩带彩纸挂在门上，求得吉祥。

行走在马六甲的街上、海边，我深深感受到中国文化对当地文化的

影响，同时也感受到当地人民对郑和的热爱。而今，中国的"一带一路"倡议，又给马六甲的发展带来了契机，希望马六甲有更加灿烂的明天，也希望它与中国人民的友谊永远长存，万古长青。

Chinese Imprint in Malacca

Yin Zihan（9 years old, Affiliated Primary School of Chengdu Normal University）

In August 2017, I had the honor to be a "little panda reporter", and participated in the Belt and Road news relaying held by Chengdu Radio and Television Station. On August 9, I arrived at the port city—Malacca.

In the old town of Malacca, around an compact area, in the middle of an old alley, there was a spectacular building with four curled-up roof corners, gray walls, scarlet pillars. On the dark brown plaque there were gilded Chinese words—Zheng He Museum. The museum was broad and bright, with Chinese wooden furniture and modern exhibition cabinet, as if you were in the Hakka community in Luodai Ancient Town in Chengdu.

Zheng He had seven expeditions to the South Seas from 1405 to 1433. The largest scale voyage of his seven voyages included a fleet of 280 ships and more than 28700 people. It was the largest fleet in the world at that time. On board there were also farm fields, vegetable fields, etc. The fleet has been

stopped for supply in Malacca for many times.

Zheng He's voyages mainly aimed at spreading Chinese culture and tradition. When Zheng He came to Malacca, Malacca was just a small fishing village. Zheng He presented Chinese porcelain, silk and tea to the Malays, and exchanged local spices, jewelry and coral with Chinese specialties. Zheng He also taught the local people how to do business and row boats on the sea to fish with nets.

Zheng He's contribution to Malacca was not forgotten by the locals. In Zheng He Museum, there were large statues of Zheng He with the King of Malaysia, Zheng He's fleet and the blue and white porcelain and Chinese medicinal materials brought by Zheng He. In the courtyard, there was still a well reserved for Zheng He. A small hill near the museum was also named Sanbao Hill in order to commemorate Zheng He.

We came to the Sanbao Temple in the mountain. The red tile walls and the lighted candles were in the typical ancient Chinese style. In the temple, there was a standing statue of Zheng He. Two of the seven wells that Zheng He and his team dug were still kept in the temple. Our guiding teacher said, in those days, crew members mainly drunk rainwater, but the rainwater was not enough, so people had to dig wells. After the wells were dug, water from the well could supply for both crew members and the local people.

In Malacca, there is also a place called Wengutang, where

the relics has witnessed the integration of Chinese people and the locals after Zheng He's trips to Malacca. Inside the hall, there was a display of applications that many Malays and Chinese used hundreds of years ago. I was attracted to a small wooden bucket with a height of more than 20 centimeters. I wondered that in such a small barrel how much water might be held. It turned out that the barrel was not for water, but for keeping money. The Malays put money in the barrel, and hung it on the beam with a rope so that it would not be taken by the children. There was a group of photos that looked familiar to me. They were lanterns and ribbons used by Chinese people during the Spring Festival. In fact, Malacca people also celebrate the Spring Festival, and also paste the colored paper on the door for luck.

Walking on the streets and seaside of Malacca, I felt the great influence of Chinese culture on the locals, and also felt the local people's love for Zheng He. Today, the Belt and Road initiative brings opportunity to the development of Malacca. I hope the Malacca has a bright future. I hope the friendship between Chine and Malaysia lasts forever.

66 出门在外，团队意识很重要。

Teamwork is very important for travelers.

99

颖墨涵

12岁

成都师范银都小学

团队意识

▲环球影城 （摄影 王磊/视界）

在学校，老师常常对我们说，要有团队意识，可我并不明白什么叫团队意识。而2017年暑假，对于身处异国他乡的14位追访一带一路"熊猫小记者"来说，团队意识就是大家必须集体行动，一个都不能少。因为作为一个团队，一旦少了一个人，或者一个人不经意的特立独行，就意味着其他人都将受到影响。

记得8月7日在新加坡环球影城时，大孩子想玩刺激些的项目，而小孩子只想坐坐小火车，我们就被临时分为两个组，一个大小孩组，一个小小孩组。我和另外5位10岁以上的小记者被分到了大孩子组，我们自行去那些刺激的活动项目前排队。

当我拍摄完大街上一辆辆陈旧的老爷车时，却发现小杨不见了。本来小杨、苗倬尔与我在一起的，现在只剩下苗倬尔了。"天呐！小杨不见了！"我叫了起来。

苗倬尔拨通了黄子函的电话："喂！黄子函，你跑哪儿去了？你和谁在一起呢？"

"我都不知道我在哪里！还有你们几个，跑哪里去啦？"黄子函的语气中充满焦急。

"这样，我们大家到古埃及那个过山车门前去集合。"

苗倬尔又给卢昱霏打了通电话："喂！卢昱霏，你在哪儿呢？你和谁在一起呢？"

"哎哟喂！我正在找你们呢！哦！我和克桑在一起呢！你们在哪儿啊？"

我们通过电话，约定了见面的地方。等所有通过电话的人都在古埃及过山车门前坐着时，我严肃地说："我们摊上大麻烦了，小杨不见了。"

找人要紧！我们分成两组，分头找人。不肯坐过山车的黄子函、克桑、卢昱霏一组，想坐过山车的我和苗倬尔一组。

为了尽快坐上过山

车，我和苗倬尔拼了！肚子饿了，忍着；脚酸了，坚持。我们走呀走，来来回回地走，估计环球影城园区几乎跑遍了，可小杨连个人影也没见着。

"算了，我们总不能为一个小杨毁了一次美好的旅行吧！"苗倬尔猫着腰，双手抱住膝盖，呼呼地喘着气，她已走不动了。

"哎！饿了吗？我们去吃东西吧！也许有心栽花花不开、无意插柳柳成荫呢！"我拉着她，向古埃及过山车对面一家餐厅的服务台走去。

匆忙之下，我们草草吃完了午饭。此时，我们又遇上了黄子函、克桑、卢昱霏，可是小杨依然没有消息。找了快三个小时了，时间已是下午一点半，大家都准备放弃寻找了。忽然，小杨出现在了我们的眼前，她正站在一家商店出口的柱子旁呆呆地看风景。

见到小杨，我们十分高兴，虽然我的过山车梦破灭了，我们已耗费了在环球影城一半的玩耍时间了，但因为我们这6朵金花是一个团队。

Team Awareness

Yan Mohan (12 years old, Affiliated Yindu Primary School of Chengdu Normal University)

In school, teachers often tell us about the teamwork, but I don't know exactly what the teamwork means. In the summer of 2017, for the 14 "little panda reporters" aboard, we finally knew that teamwork means everyone should act as one group, no one was to be left behind, because as a team, once a person was missing, or anyone was unconscious of collective action, it would cast affects on others.

On August 7, at Universal Studios in Singapore, several elder kids wanted to play trilling games, and the younger kids just wanted to sit on the train. We were temporarily divided into two groups, the elder kids group and the younger kids group. I was assigned to the elder kids group with five other elder reporters over 10 years old. We would be quelling for the thrilling games.

When I finished taking pictures on the old vintage cars on the street, I found Little Yang was missing. Little Yang, Miao and I were supposed to be together, now there was only Miao beside me. "My god! Little Yang is missing!" I cried.

Miao called Huang on the phone, "Huang, where have you been? Who are you with? "

"I don't know where I am! And you guys, where have you been?" Huang was full of anxiety.

"So, we all go to the gate of the Ancient Egypt roller coaster. We should get together."

Miao said to Lu on the phone, "Where are you, Lu? Who are you with?"

"Dear me! I'm looking for you! Oh! I'm with Ke! Where are you?"

We made an appointment by telephone. When all the people on the phone were sitting in front of the gate of the Ancient Egypt roller coaster, I said seriously, "We're in big trouble. Little Yang's missing."

It was important to find the missing one! We split up into two groups. One group were those who didn't want to sit on the roller coaster: Huang, Ke and Lu. The other one included Miao and I.

In order to get on the roller coaster as soon as possible, Miao and I tried our best to find the missing friend! We were hungry and tired after long walking. Be patient! Stick to it! We told to ourselves. We walked back and forth, and we went through almost the whole universal studios, but still could not

find Little Yang.

"Come on, we can't ruin a good trip just because of Little Yang!" Miao bent, clasped her knees and panted. She was too tired to move.

"Ah! Hungry? Let's go to eat something! Perhaps just as the saying: a watched flower never blooms, but an untended willow grows!" I took her to the front desk of a restaurant across from the ancient Egyptian roller coaster.

In a hurry, we had a quick lunch. At this time, we met Huang, Ke and Lu, but still had no news of Little Yang. Nearly three hours passed. It was half past one in the afternoon and everyone was ready to give up searching. Suddenly, Little Yang appeared in front of us. She was standing by the pillar of a shop and looking at the scenery.

My roller coaster dream was broken, and we spent half of the time searching for Little Yang at Universal Studios. We were still very happy. No matter what happened, we—"six flowers"— stayed as one team.

" "一带一路"倡议必将加深中国与沿线国家的友谊。

The Belt and Road initiative will deepen the friendship between China and countries along the route. "

苗倬尔

12岁

成都市泡桐树小学

满满的收获

2017年8月6日至11日，我作为"熊猫小记者"的一员，参加了成都市广播电视台举办的全球追访"一带一路"大型公益新闻接力行动。那郑和下西洋的故事、粉红清真寺里的祷告声至今依旧在我耳边萦绕，小伙伴们天真而快活的笑脸也时时浮现在我眼前。

8月6日，我们去了新加坡的胡姬花园。那里的胡姬花和星星棕榈树令我们着迷。更为神奇的是，如果你付给胡姬植物园几千元人民币，他们可以按你的性格与喜好研发出一种新的胡姬花，并用你的名字来命名呢！随后，我们来到新加坡的中文学校，那里的孩子们都会说一口流利的普通话，还会学着写作文、运

用成语。8月7日，我们去了环球影城。那里人头攒动，游乐设施也很先进，特别是惊险的过山车令我难忘，我们在那里度过了美好的一天。8月8日，我们来到了马来西亚的乐高乐园。那里的乐高积木建筑，向人们展示了乐高搭建的无限可能性与可塑性，是一片充满想象与创造的乐土。这些参观的景点在我眼中，都是国家与国家之间相互帮助一起进步的成果，也是当地文明进步的象征。

除了娱乐与见识国家的发展，我们也去重温了历史，增加了许多我们闻所未闻的知识。在马来西亚的三宝山上，我们看到了郑和在下西洋时打的水井；在温古堂里，我们了解了老一代马来西亚人的生活，我还学会了箍传统马来木桶的方法；在郑和博物馆里，我们清楚感受了郑和对马六甲人民生活的深远影响。

在这次活动中，我还交到了很多好朋友，很多新加坡和马来西亚的好朋友。虽然我们个性不同，但我们都一样热爱文化，乐于促进国与国之间的友好交往。我们常常在一起讨论我们当天的所见所闻，分享自己的成果，吸收他人的精华，渐渐扩充自己的知识面。

此次活动结束之后，我与新认识的新加坡朋友和马来西亚朋友，也常常通过网络交流。交到了这么多知心朋友，是我此行一个重要的收获。"一带一路"倡议的基础就是民心相通，而我与新认识的朋友，正是民心相通的组成部分。

Full Harvest

Miao Zhuoer (12 years old, Chengdu Paotongshu Primary School)

From August 6 to 11, 2017, as a member of "little panda reporters", I participated in the Belt and Road global news relay held by Chengdu Radio and Television Station. The memories still come back to me frequently— the story of Zheng He's voyages, the prayer in the Pink Mosque, and the innocent and cheerful smiling faces of my friends.

On August 6, we went to the orchid garden in Singapore. We were fascinated by the flowers and the star palm trees. What's even more amazing was that if you pay a few thousand yuan to the botanical garden, they can breed a new kind of orchid according to your personality and preference, and name it after you! Then we went to a Chinese school in Singapore where the children could speak fluent Mandarin and could learn to write essays and use Chinese idioms. On August 7, we went to universal studios. There were a lot of people there, and the recreation facility was very advanced, especially the thrilling roller coaster was unforgetable, and we had a wonderful day there. On August 8, we went to the Legoland in Malaysia. The Lego building there showed the infinite possibilities and

plasticity of blocks. It was a land of imagination and creativity. In my eyes, these scenic spots were the fruits of the cooperation between countries, and also the symbol of the progress of the local civilization.

In addition to playing and seeing how other countries develop, we also learned some history and gained a lot of knowledge we had never heard of. On the Sanbao Mountain in Malaysia, we had seen many Zheng He's wells. In Wengutang, we learned about the life of the old Malaysians, and I learned how to make the traditional Malay barrel. In Zheng He Museum, we knew the profound influence of Zheng He on the life of the Malacca people.

At the same time, in this project, I also made, many good friends of Singapore and Malaysia. Although we had different personalities, we all shared the same love for culture and were happy to promote friendly exchanges between countries. We discussed what we saw and heard, shared our achievements, learned from each other, and gradually gained knowledge.

After the journey, I often communicate with my new friends from Singapore and Malaysia via internet. It is a huge gain for me to make so many friends. The foundation of the Belt and Road initiative is people-to-people bond. And my friendship with the Singapore and Malay kids is a part of this bond.

开放的成都欢迎全世界的人们。

Chengdu opens her heart and welcomes people from all over the world.

特别采访

一次特别的采访

▲天府新区夜景 （摄影 李志勇/视界）

见到马来西亚国际贸易及工业部第二部长黄家泉是"熊猫小记者"回到成都后的事了。2017年8月14日，"熊猫小记者"听说马来西亚国际贸易及工业部第二部长黄家泉来到了成都，且使马来西亚中国馆在双流落户。"熊猫小记者"郑和队的几名代表对黄家泉部长进行了采访。

▲采访马来西亚国际贸易及工业部第二部长黄家泉（右二）

当谈到对成都的印象时，黄部长说，没来成都之前，对成都的认识是"蜀道难，难于上青天"；来了成都之后，才知道成都是"天府

▲太古里风光 （摄影 蒲圣/视界）

之国"，有着丰富的自然资源和文化资源，并且是一座文化底蕴特别深厚的城市。黄部长还说，成都不仅是文化之城，也是科技之城，全世界30％的iPad都产自成都。

黄部长还谈道，作为一个人口上千万的特大城市，成都的消费市场巨大。马来西亚出口到中国商品的前几位分别是电子产品、矿物燃料、机械和橡胶，而马来西亚一年出口到成都的商品就有10亿美元。

为了扩大成都与马来西亚的贸易，马来西亚准备参与2018年成都的科技博览会。到时，黄部长将带马来西亚的科技厂商到成都参展，希望借此与四川

▲成都宽窄巷子 （摄影 马骏聪/视界）

的厂商联合，形成生产链。同时，黄部长也将把中国的商品卖到东盟去。

在谈到马来西亚中国馆时，黄部长说，随着马来西亚

▲成都红星路步行街夜景 （摄影 刘永徽/视界）

▲成都天府广场全景 （摄影 曾伏龙/视界）

中国馆10月在双流落户，成都人可以在家门口买到原汁原味的来自马来西亚的商品，如榴莲、肉骨茶、白咖啡、燕窝等。同时，通过海铁联运的方式，成都的郫县豆瓣、火锅底料也会快速地运往马来西亚。

在谈到8月初"熊猫小记者"前去马来西亚进行交流、传播中国文化、感受马来西亚文化时，黄部长认为，"熊猫小记者"的行动，有利于保护中华传统文化，让中华文化在当地华人中落地生根。

A Special Interview

It was when "little panda reporters" came back to Chengdu that they met Mr. Huang Jiaquan, the Second Minister of International Trade and Industry in Malaysia. On August 14, 2017, "little panda reporters" got the news that Mr. Huang Came to Chengdu and had managed to set up Malaysia pavilion in Shuangliu District. Thus, several members of Zheng He Team interviewed him.

When it came to the impression of Chengdu, Mr. Huang said that before he came to Chengdu, all he knew about Chengdu was the well-known saying, "the road to Shu(Sichuan) is harder than to climb the sky". After coming to Chengdu, the city known as the "land of abundance", he found that it is with abundant natural resources, cultural resources and profound cultural heritage. At the same time, Mr. Huang noted that Chengdu was not only a city of culture, but also a city of science and technology; 30% of the world's iPad is produced in Chengdu.

In addition, Mr. Huang said that as a huge city with tens of millions of people, Chengdu's consumer market was huge. The main commodities that Malaysia exports to China are electronics, fossil fuels, machinery and rubber, while the price amounts to $1 billion annually.

To expand trade between Chengdu and Malaysia, Malaysia is preparing to participate in the science and technology exposition in Chengdu in 2018. At that time, Mr. Huang will lead Malaysian technology manufacturers to Chengdu to participate in the exhibition, hoping to join hands with the manufacturers in Sichuan to form a production chain. Meanwhile, Mr. Huang will sell Chinese goods to ASEAN.

When it comes to Malaysia pavilion, Mr. Huang said, in October, as the Malaysia pavilion in Shuangliu District being set up, people could buy the Malaysian goods, such as durian, bak kut teh, white coffee, bird's nest and so on at home. At the same time, through sea–rail combined transportation, Chengdu's Pixian Horsebean Chili Paste, hot pot sauce would also be quickly shipped to Malaysia.

When talking about the "little panda reporter" project in August, Mr. Huang thought, it's a good thing for "little panda reporters" went to Malaysia to communicate and spread Chinese culture, experienced the Malaysian culture. He also thought this project would do good to Chinese traditional culture reserve, and helped Chinese culture taking roots among oversea Chinese communities.

"熊猫小记者"郑和队2018年夏季活动照片

▲
8月3日参访越
南川渝商会 ▶
▼

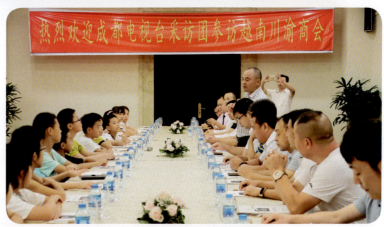

◀ 8月3日参观
老挝亚太卫
星公司

▲8月3日参观中国驻老挝大使馆

▲8月4日走进柬埔寨华商日报暹粒分社

◀ 8月5日向《吴哥微笑》团队赠送礼物

8月5日与《吴哥微笑》▶
管理团队合影

◀ 8月5日在柬埔寨暹
粒探访孤儿院

8月5日在柬埔寨暹粒向▶
孤儿赠送熊猫礼物

8月5日与暹粒孤儿▶
进行足球友谊赛

◀8月7日在柬埔寨暹粒
了解中医援助成果

8月8日在越▶
南河内感受
当地文化

▲8月7日在暹粒领事办公室

▲8月8日在中国驻柬埔寨王国大使馆暹粒领事办公室外与两位领事合影

▲8月8日在中国驻越南大使馆与文化参赞彭世团交流

▲8月8日在中国驻越南大使馆向文化参赞彭世团送熊猫玩偶

▲8月8日在中国驻越南大使馆与文化参赞彭世团合影

第四章

冬季活动——"中国年·成都行"

Chapter Four
Winter Session—"Trip to Chengdu in Chinese New Year"

"中国年·成都行"活动简介

"熊猫小记者"全球追访"一带一路"大型公益新闻接力行动第一季（冬季活动）于2018年2月13—19日（中国农历新年）在成都举行。本次活动邀请了来自西班牙、德国、法国、匈牙利、波兰、俄罗斯、加拿大、澳大利亚、哈萨克斯坦、越南等10个"一带一路"相关国家的"熊猫小记者"家庭，他们与成都志愿者家庭一起，体验新天府文化，感受成都发展，欢度成都味中国年。这次国外"熊猫小记者"中国年成都行活动，以国际视野精心策划，制造话题，形成热点，引导舆论；以别出心裁的方式宣传天府文化，传播成都形象，取得了良好的口碑和社会反响。

在2月13—19日为期一周的时间里，国外"熊猫小记者"家庭与成都志愿者家庭一起逛庙会、赏花灯、游名胜古迹、品成都美食，游览成都新地标。从成都大熊猫繁育研究基地、都江堰、杜甫草堂、武侯祠到金沙遗址博物馆、永陵博物馆，从成都国际铁路港到玉林社区居民新年游乐活动，独具魅力的天府文化、地道的成都新年，让每一位国外"熊猫小记者"都对成都深度融入"一带一路"建设、构筑国家对外开放门户枢纽有了直观而真实的感受，他们对成都的速度与温度、成都普通市民的热情与友善都给予了高度的评价。通过这次活动，搭建起了中外文化

交流、文明互鉴的友谊桥梁，每一位国外"熊猫小记者"及家人纷纷表示爱上了成都，希望下次要和自己的朋友再来成都，来自西班牙的"熊猫小记者"家庭甚至希望到成都居住生活。

本次国外"熊猫小记者"中国年成都行活动自开展以来，受到中央电视台、中央人民广播电台、《中国日报》等国内主流媒体的高度关注，不惜时间与版面主动加以报道。新华网、人民网、中新网、央视网、央广网、新浪、网易、搜狐等新媒体持续关注活动进展。2月14日的央视《新闻联播》报道了此次活动；2月15日上午，央视综合频道、新闻频道对本次活动进行了长达10分钟的并机直播；央视中文国际频道《中国新闻》连续3天对国外"熊猫小记者"的活动进行了跟踪报道。此外，《四川日报》《华西日报》《成都日报》《成都商报》、四川电视台、成都电视台、四川新闻网、四川观察、看度、一头条、成都全搜索等本土报纸、电视、网站及其他新媒体都关注报道了本次活动。《四川日报》在节后第一天以一个整版的图片回顾了本次活动。截至目前，国内近百家媒体报道了此次活动，共计刊发报道100余篇，其中新华社、《人民日报》、央视等中央级媒体报道近10篇，对推广天府文化、传播成都形象起到了良好的传播效果，从而提升了成都的知名度、美誉度。

Brief Introduction to Project of "Trip to Chengdu in Chinese New Year"

The second season of the "little panda reporter" global follow-up "the Belt and Road" news relaying was held in Chengdu on February 13 to 19, 2018 (Chinese New Year). This activity invited "little panda reporters" from countries along the Road including Spain, Germany, France, Hungary, Poland, Russia, Canada, Australia, Kazakhstan and Vietnam. They were invited to Chengdu to stay in volunteers' homes, to experience culture of the Land of Abundance, to feel the development of Chengdu, and to celebrate Chinese Spring Festival. This time, the foreign "little panda reporters" project was elaborately planed and well-organized with an international view, it aroused hot discussion and public attention. The culture of the Land of Abundance is publicized in an innovative way and the glamour of Chengdu is showed splendidly. This project was a huge success which achieved good reputation and active public reaction.

During February 13 to 19, foreign "little panda reporters" stayed at homes of Chengdu local family for one week. Together they went to temple fair, admiring the lanterns, they visited scenic spots, historical sites and new landmarks of Chengdu, tasted Chengdu food. From Chengdu Research Base of Giant Panda Breeding, Dujiangyan Irrigation System, Du Fu's Thatched Cottage, Wuhou Temple, Jinsha Museum and Yonglin Museum, from Chengdu International Railway Port to Yulin community residents recreation activities in the New Year, the unique charm of culture, the authentic Chengdu New Year's day, make every "little panda reporter" feel in person the Belt and Road construction, the construction of national portal opening hub in Chengdu. They sang the praises of Chengdu's convenience and efficiency, the hospitality of Chengdu citizens. This activity is a bridge of friendship towards cultural exchanges and mutual learning. Each foreign "little panda reporter" and the family members fell in love with Chengdu. They hoped next time to come back to Chengdu with friends. One Spain family even expressed their willingness to live in Chengdu.

This project of foreign "little panda reporters" covering Chengdu during Chinese new year attracted attention of domestic mass media such as CCTV, CNR, *China Daily*, etc. The medium spared no effort to cover the story. Xinhuanet, Peoplenet, Chinanews, CCTV, CNR, Sina, Netease, Sohu and other new media continue to focus on the progress of the activity. The event was reported by *Network News Broadcast* on CCTV on February 14. On the morning of February 15, CCTV Comprehensive Channel and News Channel conducted a 10-minute live broadcast of the event. *China News* of CCTV's Chinese-language International Channel has been tracking the activities of foreign "little panda reporters" for three consecutive days. In addition, local influential newspapers, TV, websites and new media all covered the story, such as *Sichuan Daily, Huaxi Daily, Chengdu Daily, Chengdu Economic Daily,* Sichuan TV Station, Chengdu TV Station, Sichuan News Net, Sichuan Observe, Cando, Headline, Chengdu Search, etc. *Sichuan Daily* reviewed the event on the first day of the festival with a full-page picture. So far, a total of more than 100 pieces of news about the activities were reported by domestic media, among which nearly 10 were reported by national news agencies including Xinhua News Agency, *People's Daily* and CCTV. The local culture of Sichuan, the image and reputation of Chengdu are thus promoted and communicated excellently.

　　2018年2月16日，中国农历新年的大年初一，国外"熊猫小记者"团队来到成都天府新区华阳街道办事处，感受了一系列由南山社区和菜蔬社区精心组织的"亲老、敬老、爱老"活动。

　　孩子们的到来，让原本安静的社区养老中心瞬间热闹了起来。学说中文拜年祝福语、写春联、包饺子、画糖饼，来自国内外的30多个家庭，与一暄康养社区养老中心的爷爷奶奶们共同度过了一个快乐、温馨、祥和的春节。通过此次活动，孩子们更加深刻理解了尊老敬老这一中华民族的传统美德。

此外，小记者们还在位于天府新区华阳街道办事处的海昌极地海洋公园观看了海豚表演，学习海洋文化、了解保护海洋生态环境的重要性。

▲ 接待哈萨克斯坦与西班牙家庭
的成都小朋友拿着摄像机争当小记者

▲ 在金沙博物馆感受中国
文化，并吃着自己转得的糖饼

▲哈萨克斯坦小记者、俄罗斯小记者与成都小朋友很快成为好朋友

▲在金沙博物馆参加"熊猫小记者"启动仪式

▲澳大利亚小记者、西班牙小记者与成都小朋友在都江堰

▲西班牙小记者、成都接待家庭的小朋友、加拿大小记者在苏宁易购

▲国外"熊猫小记者"和中国志愿者接待家庭在苏宁易购外合影

▲俄罗斯小记者、哈萨克斯坦小记者和成都接待家庭的小朋友到苏宁易购
采购年货

▲哈萨克斯坦小记者和俄罗斯小记者的妈妈在金沙遗址

来自西班牙的

安

An En La Ruta De La Seda

Me llamo 安, y tengo 6 años. Me gusta hablar chino con mis amigas chinas y con mi padre, pero nunca había oído hablar de la ruta de la seda hasta hace 2 semanas.

La primera vez que fui a China iba en la barriga de mi madre. Cuando nací, una chica que se llama Hongyi me cantaba muy bien canciones chinas en sus brazos. También les aclaró a mis padres el significado y lo que representa mi nombre en chino "安".

Cuando me faltaba poco para cumplir 3 años, conocí a Renle y Feifei, que son de Chendu. Un día que volvieron de Chendu en vacaciones, me regalaron un cuadro de un oso panda con mi nombre en chino. Ocasionalmente, también como con ellos comida picante de Chengdu.

Ahora hace 4 años que empecé a estudiar chino en una escuela de niños chinos nacidos en Barcelona. Además, en mi colegio catalán también he organizado proyectos sobre China. Por ejemplo, canté a mis compañeras una canción en chino que se titula "jazmín", les mostré ropa tradicional de seda china, comida china, y también el mapa de China para que supieran donde están los osos panda.

Ahora voy a ir a Chengdu para ser una Osita Panda Periodista. Por este motivo, mi profesora me ha dicho que explique este evento a mis compañeras. Por lo tanto, empecé a documentarme y a entender el concepto de la Ruta de la Seda. Por ejemplo, voy a explicar que hace mucho mucho tiempo unas personas chinas salían a caballo o en barco desde sitios como Qingbaijiang, y traían ropa de seda, faldas y otros productos a diferentes países de Europa y a Barcelona. Entonces, se llevaban productos de aquí para China. Naturalmente, ahora ya no vienen con caballos; vienen con trenes, camiones y barcos.

El sábado pasado, cuando salí de chino, Renle y Feife me enseñaron comida que había venido de Chengdu desde Qingbaijiang: pasta de Chengdu, brotes de bambú, pimientos para hacer Olla Picante de Chengdu, etcétera... Más tarde, también fuimos a ver un musical titulado Silk, the Ethernal Road. Me gustó mucho porque era sobre la Ruta de la Seda, y eran cantantes chinos, niñas y niños de una escuela primaria. Me gustó especialmente una escena en la que las actrices se liaban un pañuelo de seda juntos en el brazo y viajaban en el tiempo por la ruta de la seda.

Gracias a la invitación de la Televisión de Chengdu, pronto voy a conocer el principio de la ruta de la seda.

安的"一带一路"

安（西班牙）

我叫安，今年6岁啦。我喜欢和我的中国朋友，还有我的爸爸说中文。但是，直到两周前我才第一次听说"一带一路"。

我第一次去中国的时候还在妈妈肚子里呢。当我出生的时候，一个叫虹邑的女孩特别喜欢把我抱在她温暖的怀里唱着好听的中文歌。她还告诉我的爸爸妈妈，我中文名字中"安"所代表的含义。

当我快3岁的时候，认识了来自成都的任乐和菲菲。有一次他们从成都回来时给我带了一张有我中文名字"安"的熊猫画。偶尔，我还会和他们一起去吃辣辣的成都菜呢。

4年前，我开始去中文学校上中文课了。而且，在我的加泰兰学校里我也参加了很多和中国有关的活动。比如，我给我的同学们唱中文歌曲《茉莉花》，向他们介绍中国丝绸衣服、中国的食物，还在中国地图上帮他们找到了熊猫在哪里呢。

现在我要去成都当"熊猫小记

▲西班牙小记者安拿着摄像机说自己是真正的"熊猫小记者"

▲西班牙家庭与成都志愿者家庭品尝成都"坝坝宴"

者"啦！为此，我的老师约兰达让我向我的同学介绍情况。于是，我开始了解有关"一带一路"的点点滴滴。比如，我要向我的同学介绍，在很久很久以前，古代的中国人骑马或坐船从青白江出发，把用丝绸做的衣服、裙子及其他物品运到欧洲各个地方，包括巴塞罗那。然后呢，他们又会把当地的东西带回中国。当然，现在他们不会骑着马来了，他们会用火车、卡车或者船舶运输过来。

上个星期六我上完中文课之后，任乐和菲菲带我去了一个中国超市，向我介绍了许多从青白江运送过来的成都的食品，有面、竹笋、做火锅的辣椒等。随后，我们又去看了《丝路永恒》音乐剧。我非常喜欢这个音乐剧，因为它是关于"一带一路"的，而且演员们都来自中国北京的一个小学。我特别喜欢其中的一幕，小演员们用丝绸做的手绢将手臂捆绑在一起，畅游在丝绸之路上。

在此，非常感谢成都市广播电视台的邀请，我即将去认识"一带一路"的起点啦！

▲西班牙"熊猫小记者"安与成都接待小朋友在成都
铁路港分享蓉欧汇里买到的酸奶

266

来自澳大利亚的

亚瑟·王·洛佩斯

267

"The Belt and Road" and Me

Arthur Wang Lopes (Australia)

My name is Arthur Wang Lopes, in Chinese my first name means "King Arthur". I got this name from my mother and she is Chinese. She was born in China and moved to Australia. My dad was born in Brazil and grew up in America. I was born in Australia and my sister was born in America. We are a family from 4 different continents: Asia, South America, Oceania and North America. Now we all live together in Melbourne. We are a "global family" literally and we travel around the world to many different countries when we are on holidays. We went to Spain and Italy in 2016, everywhere we went, we met a lot of Chinese people! The world is connected, and if we don't travel to another country, we can use Internet to talk and see other family members. I often talk to my grandma in America and grandpa in Brazil on the Internet during the weekend.

I heard about the story of the Silk Road, which was a road to connect different countries in ancient time. Now we can fly to different countries in airplane very quickly instead of travelling on the road. I have travelled to many cities in many countries since I was born. For example, I have been to China, America, Canada, Australia, Germany, Denmark, Spain and Italy. I have experienced many different types of culture and tried different food. Sichuan spicy food is one of the favourite food for my parents, but it is too spicy for me. I like the non-spicy Chinese food, like dumplings, noodle and much other Chinese food that my Chinese grandparents make for us.

When we travelled to different countries, we found people speak different languages. I have been learning Chinese since I was born and learning Portuguese as well. I learned a little bit French and Spanish in the school. If I know the language then it is easy for me to understand and talk to people in their languages. Chinese is very difficult to learn and I am still learning how to "draw" Chinese characters and how to speak Mandarin. I learned pinyin in the school which could help me to pronounce the characters. I like some of the Chinese stories and especially like the dragon stories, and the stories of "zao wang ye" which happens during the Chinese Lunar New Year.

The world is connected, but many things are made in China. My mum always jokes that she is also "made in China". We have a lot of toys, books and clothes which are all from China. My sister has her "qi pao" from China too. We live in Australia now and my dad always says we are far away from everyone in the world. In Australia, you can find many Chinese things everywhere and I go to attend Chinese school on the weekend. I have been to China when I was very little and I like to go again to the places I have never been to.

I like to tell stories what I have seen during the trips to my friends and I still remember a lot of places and things, but often I get confused. My mum often asks us to write journals when we travel and draw what we see, so we can look at them again. I read a lot of books and look at many pictures of places. It will be good to see them in real, and I think it will be fun to share stories with my school friends.

Chengdu is a place I have heard about but I have never visited. I saw giant Panda's pictures and knew they like eating bamboo, but I have never seen a real one yet. Maybe I have seen one in a zoo, but I really don't remember it at all. I like to see the real giant panda and take some pictures and videos to show to my friends. My mum told me a lot of things about Sichuan apart from the spicy food and giant pandas. I know there will be a lot of celebration during the Chinese Lunar New Year and a lot of parties. I can tell people my stories and how I travel around the world, and I can learn their stories. I want to make friends there and we can play together. I hope they have interesting playgrounds. Maybe I can learn some piano pieces from the Chinese friends there.

During the trip to Chengdu, I want to take a lot of pictures and hopefully my parents will give me a real camera to take pictures. I can upload them and make my version of pictures and take videos. I will email them to my grandparents and my sister. Maybe I can also draw a world map with my version of the Silk Road story.

我和"一带一路"

亚瑟·王·洛佩斯（澳大利亚）

　　我叫亚瑟·王·洛佩斯，在中文中，我的名字是"王亚瑟"。名字是妈妈取的，她是中国人，生于中国，后移居澳大利亚。我的爸爸出生在巴西，在美国长大。我出生在澳大利亚，妹妹则出生在美国。我们一家四口出生在四大洲：亚洲、南美洲、大洋洲和北美洲。现在我们都住在墨尔本。我们可谓是"全球大家庭"，度假也是满世界旅行。2016年我们去了西班牙和意大利，那里到处都会遇到中国人！世界是相通的，即便不出国，我们也可以通过互联网和其他家庭成员交流。周末的时候，我经常与在美国的奶奶和在巴西的爷爷视频聊天。

　　我听说过丝绸之路，它是古代连接不同国家的道路。现在我们不用跋山涉水，坐飞机就能很快到达别的国家。自从我出生以来，去过许多国家和城市。我去过中国、美国、加拿大、澳大利亚、德国、丹麦、西班牙和意大利。我感受过多种不同的文化，尝过各种不同的食物。川菜

▲澳大利亚小记者王亚瑟与成都小朋友热烈相拥

是我父母最喜欢的食物之一，但对我来说太辣了。我喜欢那些不辣的中国菜，还有饺子、面条等食物，外公外婆还给我们做了其他很多中国菜。

到各国旅行时，我们发现人们讲不同的语言。我从出生起就学习中文，也学习葡萄牙语。我在学校里学了一点法语和西班牙语。如果我懂一门语言，那么就可以用这门语言与当地人进行交流，也容易理解当地的风土人情。汉语很难，我还在学习如何"画"汉字、如何说汉语。我在学校里学会了拼音，可以用拼音拼读汉字。我喜欢中国的故事，尤其喜欢龙的传说和与春节有关的灶王爷的故事。

世界是相通的。我发现全世界都有很多中国制造的东西。我妈妈总是开玩笑说她也是"中国制造"。我们有很多玩具、图书、衣服都来自中国，包括妹妹的"旗袍"。我们现在住在澳大利亚，我爸爸总是说这是个孤岛，而实际上你可以在任何地方找到很多中国元素。我周末去上中文学校。我很小的时候就去过中国，可我还

想再去，去那些我以前没有去过的地方。

我喜欢对朋友讲我的旅途见闻，我还记得很多地方和事情，但常常搞混。我妈妈让我们写旅行日记，或把我们看到的东西画下来，这样我们就可以重新唤起美好的回忆。我看了很多书，看了很多风景照，希望能看到实景并和同学们分享。

我听说过成都，但从未去过。我见过大熊猫的照片，知道它们喜欢吃竹子，但我从来没见过真正的大熊猫。也许以前在动物园里见过，可我真的不记得了。我想看真正的大熊猫，并把照片和视频给我的朋友看。除了麻辣的食物和大熊猫，妈妈还告诉我很多关于四川的事情。我知道在中国，春节期间会举办很多新年庆祝活动和晚会。我可以告诉人们我的故事，以及我是如何环游世界的，我也可以了解他们的故事。我想在那里交朋友，和他们一起玩，我希望那里有运动场。也许中国朋友可以教我弹钢琴。

在去成都的旅途中，我想拍很多照片，希望我的父母能送我一个真正的相机。我可以上传照片，拍摄视频，编辑自己的版本。我会发电子邮件给我的祖父母和我的妹妹。也许我还可以画一幅"我眼中的丝绸之路"的世界地图。

来自匈牙利的

安戈尔·弗迪塔斯

Soha nem voltak olyan jók, hatékonyak és eredményesek a Magyarország és Kína közötti kapcsolatok, mint most. *Gazdaság*

A közép-európai régióban a Kína felé irányuló magyar export a legnagyobb különösen jelentős az exporttevékenység **az agrárium területén**. Számos agráripari-termékeket exportálunk, például borokat. Mintegy 11 ezer hektoliter magyar bor – köztük villányi borok is – jut Kínában, és ezzel Kína a negyedik legnagyobb célországunk e területen.

Az elmúlt években **4,2 milliárd dollárnyi kínai befektetés jelent meg Magyarországon**, ami azt jelenti, hogy a legmagasabb technológiai színvonalon termelő és szolgáltató vállalatok érkeztek, amelyek magyar emberek ezreinek adnak munkát. Ezek közé tartozik a **Huawei Technologies Hungary** is, melynek Európai Ellátó Központja új egységet hozott létre a Pécshez közeli **Cserkúton** 2012-ben.

A Pécsi Tudományegyetem nemzetközi stratégiájának egyik fő irányvonala az ázsiai egyetemi kapcsolatok fejlesztése, ezen belüli kiemelten fontos a kínai egyetemekkel való sokrétű együttműködések elősegítése. **A PTE ennek szellemében évek óta keresi az együttműködési lehetőségeket kínai partnerekkel, és a Nanjing Audit University-vel sikeres kapcsolatépítés indult be.** Ennek egyik eredménye a kínai-magyar kulturális és kutatóközpont, melynek ünnepélyes megnyitójára 2014-ben került sor.

2015-ben a Pécsi Tudományegyetem és a kínai Hebei United Egyetem együttműködésével nyílt Konfuciusz Intézet a hagyományos kínai orvoslás megismerésére Pécsett.

A Pécsi Konfuciusz Intézet a világon a hetedik, ami hagyományos kínai orvoslással foglalkozik. **Magyarországon** az ELTE Konfuciusz intézet, a Szegedi Konfuciusz Intézet és a Miskolci Konfuciusz Intézet után **a negyedik Konfuciusz Intézetként jött létre**. Megalapítása erősíti a két oldal közötti párbeszédet és együttműködést a kínai orvoslás területén, és elősegíti, hogy a Pécsen és vonzáskörzetében élő emberek kínaiul tanulhassanak és megismerjék a kínai kultúrát.

Kínai-magyar kapcsolatok önkormányzati területen is léteznek. **2014-ben írták alá a kínai népköztársasági Chengdu és Pécs város önkormányzatai közötti együttműködési megállapodást.** Ennek értelmében a felek tájékoztatják egymást a városaikban megrendezésre kerülő kiemelt fontosságú eseményekről, törekszenek a cserekapcsolatok megerősítésére, csereprogramokat szerveznek.

The Relationship between Hungary and China Have Reached a New Level

Angol Fordítás（Hungary）

The relations between Hungary and China have never been as good, efficient and effective as they are now. In the Central European region, exports to China are the most significant export activity in the field of agriculture. We export many agro-industrial products, such as wines. About 11000 hectoliters of Hungarian wine, including Villány wines, are in China, making China our fourth largest destination in this area.

Over the past few years, $4.2 billion of Chinese investment in Hungary has been announced, which means that Chinese producing and supplying companies with advanced technologies provide jobs for thousands of Hungarians. These include Huawei Technologies Hungary, whose European Supply Center has created a new unit in Cserkút, near Pécs in 2012.

One of the main directions of the international strategy of the University of Pécs is the development of Asian university relations, and it is particularly important to promote multilateral cooperation with Chinese universities.

PTE has for years been looking for cooperation opportunities with Chinese partners, and successful networking with Nanjing Audit University has started. One of the results is the Sino–Hungarian Cultural and Research Center, whose solemn opening ceremony took place in 2014.

In 2015, the Confucius Institute, with the collaboration of the University of Pécs and the Chinese Hebei United University, opened up the traditional Chinese medicine in Pécs.

The Confucius Institute in Pécs is the seventh in the world, which deals with traditional Chinese medicine, after the Confucius Institute of ELTE, the Confucius Institute in Szeged and the Confucius Institute in Miskolc, was established as the fourth Confucius Institute in Hungary. Its founding strengthens dialogue and cooperation between the two sides in Chinese medicine and promotes people living in Pécs and their neighborhoods to learn Chinese and learn about Chinese culture.

Chinese–Hungarian relations also exist in the local government area. In 2014, the Co–operation Agreement between the Chengdu of the People's Republic of China and Pécs Municipalities was signed. Accordingly, the parties will inform each other of the events of major importance in their cities, strive to strengthen exchanges and organize exchanges.

匈中友好关系迈上新台阶

安戈尔·弗迪塔斯（匈牙利）

匈牙利与中国的关系从未像今天这样友好、高效、密切。中欧地区农产品最主要的出口对象是中国。我们出口大量工农业产品，如葡萄酒等。匈牙利出口到中国的葡萄酒大约1.1万升，包括维拉尼葡萄酒，中国成为匈牙利第四大葡萄酒市场。

▲匈牙利布达佩斯 （摄影 刘杰/视界）

据称，近几年中国在匈牙利投资达42亿美元。通过中国生产商和供应商的投资，引进了先进的技术，为匈牙利人提供了成千上万的工作机会。其中包括中国驻匈牙利的华为技术公司。2012年，其欧洲供应中心在佩奇附近的切尔库特建立了一个新的分部。

匈牙利佩奇大学国际化战略的主要方向之一是谋求与亚洲高校关系的发展，尤为重要的是促进与中国高校的多边合作。多年来，佩奇大学一直在寻找与中国伙伴的合作机会，并与南京审计大

▲成都接待家庭和来自匈牙利的朋友在武侯祠

学建立了良好的关系。合作成果之一是共同建立中匈文化研究中心，该中心于2014年隆重开幕。

2015年，佩奇大学和中国河北联合大学合作成立了孔子学院，还开设了中医药研究中心（或分部）。

佩奇孔子学院是世界上第七所孔子学院,且可进行中医药研究，也是继罗兰大学、塞格德大学和米什科尔茨大学的孔子学院之后，在匈牙利成立的第四所孔子学院。佩奇孔子学院的成立加强了中匈双方在中医药方面的交流与合作，促进了佩奇当地民众学习汉语和了解中国文化。

中国和匈牙利地方政府部门也开展积极合作。2014年，双方签署了《中华人民共和国成都市与匈牙利佩奇市合作协议》。根据协议，双方将相互通报各自城市的重大事件，致力于加强与组织双边交流。

来自波兰的
库巴

Mój pogląd- „jeden pas, jedna droga „

Nazywam się Kuba , w tym roku kończę 14 lat. Jestem z Łodzi, obecnie jestem uczniem szkoły gimnazjalnej o kierunku piłki nożnej. Moim marzeniem jest zostanie profesjonalnym piłkarzem, takim jakim jest np. Robert Lewandowski.

Jakiś czas temu otrzymałem radosną informację , że dostaniemy wraz z moją rodziną zaproszenia od CDTV. Będziemy mieli możliwość spędzenia Nowego Roku w Chinach. Mamy też możliwość mieszkania u lokalnej, ale niestety moja młodsza siostra jest zbyt mała do podróży. Musi zostać z mamą , a ja jedynie mogę kupić jej prezent w trakcie wyjazdu.

Pierwszy raz o projekcie **„jeden pas, jedna droga"** usłyszałem w telewizji , wtedy dowiedziałem się , że z Chengdu są wysyłane towary drogą kolejową przez ok. 10 dni. Jak tylko zdobyłem tę informację zapytałem taty czy możemy jechać pociągiem do Chin. Dopiero później zrozumiałem , że jest to pociąg towarowy i nie mamy możliwości skorzystania z jego usług. Bardzo często spotykałem w późniejszym czasie na swojej drodze ludzi, którzy z buzi przypominali chińczyków, ale oni chyba jedynie przyjeżdżali do Łodzi na spotkania biznesowe. Najczęściej z tego co zdarzyłem zaobserwować mieli oni restauracje w których mieliśmy okazje zjeść , jednak mam nadzieję, że jednak w Chinach będziemy mieli możliwość spróbowania dań tamtejszego rejonu w typowo chińskich restauracjach.

Moja rodzina prowadzi biznes w Polsce. Mój dziadek , babcia , ciocia , tata prowadzą jedną firmą. Z ich opowieści wiem , że mamy dużo maszyn sprowadzanych własnie z Chin. Również kilka razy do roku moi Dziakowie odwiedzają ten kraj. Za każdym razem dziadek przywozi dla mnie i dla mojego rodzeństwa prezent produkowany własnie tam. Uważam , że on bardzo lubi ten naród i ten kraj. Ja niestety z powodu mojej nauki nie mam okazji by polecieć wraz z nim . Mimo to przez Internet dużo czytałem na temat Chin np. że Chiny chca rozwijać swój biznes na wschodzie , wtedy inne kraje mogły by kupować ich towar , jak również sprzedawać im swój na zasadzie wymiany. Tak samo jak teraz Chiny założyli kurs towarowo-kolejowy żeby sprzedać konkurencyjny towar dla świata , żeby inni mieli możliwość jego sprzedazy w swoich krajach. Myślę, że to dlatego Chiny są tak silnym narodem.

Cieszę się , że mamy możliwość spędzenia Nowego Roku w Chinach, gdzie będziemy mogli poznać kulturę tego kraju, posmakować chińską kuchnię, zobaczyć wiele nowych , a jednocześnie ciekawych miejsc . Ja z tatą i bratem już nie możemy się doczekać na ten wyjazd. Codziennie patrzymy na kalendarz, by ten czas do wyjazdu szybko minął, byśmy mogli już tam być. Jednocześnie mam nadzieję, że w Chengdu będę miał możliwość poznania dużo nowych znajomych żebym w przyszłości mógł ich zaprosić do Łodzi na wycieczkę.

Mała gwiazda piłki nożnej : Kuba

01.2018

我心目中的"一带一路"

库巴（波兰）

　　我叫库巴，今年14岁，来自波兰罗兹，现在是一名中学生，也是一名专业足球后备队员，我的愿望是成为一名专业的足球运动员，就像波兰的球星莱万多夫斯基一样。

　　前不久，我听爸爸说我们家非常幸运地接到了成都市广播电视台的邀请，可以到成都去过中国的新年，还能住在成都当地人的家里。听到这个消息我非常开心，只是遗憾我妹妹还太小，妈妈要留下来照顾她，不能和我们一起去，不过我们会给她们带礼物回来的。

　　我最早听到"一带一路"这个词是从我们罗兹的电视新闻里，当时好像是说有来自成都的货运列车满载着货物经过10多天的时间来到罗兹。我当时还问了爸爸，我说："这下我们也可以坐火车到中国去了！"不过后来才听说那是货运火车，不可以坐人的。从那以后，我就经常在路上看到很多穿西服的中国人，他们好像是来罗兹开会的。再后来就是罗兹又开了好几家新的中餐厅，我和我的家人都去吃过，味道还不错，但我总觉得去中国吃到的中餐会更地道吧。

　　我家人是做贸易生意的，我的爷爷奶奶和爸爸妈妈还有姑姑都在公司工作。听他们说我们有很多机械设备都是从中国采购的，而且我爷爷奶奶每年都会去中国很多次，每次回来都会给我和我的弟弟妹妹带很多中国的礼物。我的家人好像很喜欢中国，但是因为要上学的原因我还没去过，不过在网上我也看过很多有关中国的信息，比如在很早很早以前，不记得是中国的哪个朝代，中国因为希望向西发展，就慢慢地走出国门，带着中国的丝绸和其他的好东西到西方国家和他们交换，然后赚了很多钱，回去的时候还把沿途国家的一些好东西带回了中国。就和现在的情况差不多，通过中国的中欧班列，把中国的优势产品销售到不同的国家，返程的时候又把那些国家的好东西带回中国。我想，这就是中国强大的原因吧。

　　这次我们真的非常幸运，可以到中国去过年，可以真正地去了解中国的文化，品尝中国的美食，看到很多新的东西。我和爸爸及弟弟都非常激动，已经有点等不及要去中国了，每天都在看日历，希望时间快一点到来，这样我们就可以马上去中国了。同时我也希望能在成都认识更多新的小朋友，以后我也可以邀请他们到我们罗兹来玩。

来自哈萨克斯坦的

阿莱

Чэнду, жди меня!

Меня зовут Арай. Мне 11 лет. Я приехала из Казахстана. У меня небольшая семья: мама, два брата и я. Я много чем увлекаюсь: люблю рисовать, читать книги и петь. Также я очень люблю изучать языки и мечтаю стать полиглотом. Я хорошо говорю на казахском, русском и английском языках. А недавно начала изучать китайский язык.

Мне очень нравится китайский язык, на мой взгляд, он очень красивый и мелодичный. Мое первое знакомство с ним произошло благодаря моей маме. Мою маму зовут Сауле, я давно привыкла, что все ее называют Сауле лаоши, так как она работает преподавателем китайского языка в институте Конфуция. Поэтому, первым китайским словом, которое я запомнила, было "老师". Как я уже говорила, я с детства занимаюсь пением, и китайские песни пришлись мне по душе. Коллеги мамы называли меня "孔院小歌手"(маленький голос института Конфуция), потому что я часто выступала у них на концертах с такими песнями, как 《鲁冰花》,《如果感到幸福你就拍拍手》 и др.

В Китае я не впервые. Четыре года назад я с мамой уже приезжала в Китай, в город Урумчи и Или. Стремительное развитие Китая, трудолюбие и оптимизм китайцев, живописная природа и вкусная еда произвели на меня огромное впечатление.

Я бы очень хотела узнать о Китае больше, и, к счастью, у меня появилась такая возможность. От мысли, что совсем скоро я вживую увижу панд, вместе с китайскими семьями здесь, в Чэнду, встречу Новый год и познакомлюсь с ребятами со всего мира, я прихожу в неописуемый восторг.

Интересно, а что вы знаете о моей родине кроме нашего Президента Н.А.Назарбаева, Экспо-2017, и Димаш (迪玛希)? С собой в Чэнду я привезла много информации о Казахстане, много сувениров и подарков, а также национальный костюм. Позже я бы хотела рассказать вам о живописной природе, величайших горах, гостеприимных людях и многом другом, и думаю, после моего рассказа, вы точно полюбите Казахстан так же, как я люблю Китай!

Казахстан и Китай - дружественные соседние страны. Алматы , в котором я родилась, в прошлом был одним из важных центров на Великом Шелковом пути. Будучи маленькой журналисткой, я подробно изучила, что же такое "один пояс - один путь", какую роль он играет в экономике стран-участниц и др. Я узнала, что это - современный Великий Шелковый путь, который объединяет Запад и Восток и способствует их взаимовыгодному сотрудничеству и совместному развитию. Я думаю, что все мы, приехавшие из разных уголков мира, встретились здесь как раз для укрепления дружбы между нашими странами.

Я верю, что мое будущее обязательно будет связано с Китаем, После окончания школы я мечтаю поступить в ВУЗ Китая, а после работать во благо двух наших стран.

Я жду не дождусь когда мы отправимся в путешествие по городу. Чэнду, жди меня!

2018春节，我和成都有约

阿莱（哈萨克斯坦）

我叫阿莱，来自哈萨克斯坦，今年11岁。我家里有四口人：妈妈、两个哥哥和我。读书、唱歌、画画是我的最爱。另外，我还有较高的语言天赋，精通哈萨克语和俄语，会说英语，不久前又开始学习汉语，将来我要做一个通晓多种语言的人。

我喜欢汉语，是因为汉字很美，而且汉语发音像唱歌。我与汉语的缘分来自母亲，她是孔子学院的本土教师，教汉语已有十多个年头了，妈妈常开玩笑说她的桃李已经满哈萨克斯坦了。记得跟妈妈出去时，经常遇到学生称呼她"Saule老师"，所以我学的第一个汉语单词就是"老师"。学唱中文歌是我学习语言的好方法之一，参加孔子学院的晚会时，我唱过《鲁冰花》《如果感到幸福你就拍拍手》等歌曲，妈妈的同事亲切地叫我"孔院小歌手"。

4年前，我去了中国，到过乌鲁木齐和伊犁。中国的飞速发展、中国人的勤劳乐观以及中国的美景美食等都给我留下了很深的印象。这次有幸入选"熊猫小记者"活动，是让我近距离了解中国、了解成都的好机会。一想到可以亲眼见到大熊猫，可以与中国家庭一起欢度春节，可以结识来自世界各地的小朋友，我好激动哟！

人们对于哈萨克斯坦的了解可能

仅限于知道我们的总统纳扎尔巴耶夫先生、2017年的阿斯塔纳专项世博会、走红中国的歌手迪玛希。这次我准备了关于家乡的各种资料，带上我的民族服装、礼物和特产，打算向中国朋友介绍我美丽的家乡和善良好客的哈萨克斯坦人民，相信他们一定会感兴趣并喜欢，就像我喜欢中国一样。

哈萨克斯坦和中国是友好邻邦，我的出生地阿拉木图市是古丝绸之路上的重要枢纽城市。作为"熊猫小记者"，为了去成都参加这次活动，我做了一些功课，上网了解了什么是"一带一路"和新丝绸之路经济带，它能给周边国家带

来什么好处等。依据我的理解,两个国家要想在经济上互惠互利并且共同发展,首先得民心相通,我想我们这些来自世界各地的友好小使者和家庭被邀请去成都,就是为了增进友谊,促进各国的民间交流与往来。

▲哈萨克斯坦小记者阿莱在玉林天府文化年现场感受蜀绣

相信我的未来一定是和中国有关系的,我梦想去中国读大学,长大后为哈中友谊做一些力所能及的事情。

2018春节,我和成都有一个美丽的约会。

小伙伴们,"有朋自远方来"啰,不见不散!

来自法国的
龙阳

Mon point de vue sur la Ceinture et la Route

Bonjour,

Je m'appelle Yanis Laine et mon nom chinois est Long Yang. J'ai 8 ans bientôt et j'habite une petite ville a côté de Lyon en France. Je suis en classe de CE1, j'adore jouer au foot, c'est mon sport favori, et j'aime aussi jouer aux jeux vidéo.

Le week-end dernier, le 7 Janvier, nous avons fêté l'Epiphanie chez mon papi et pour l'occasion nous avons mangé la fameuse galette des rois. Il y a la télévision dans la cuisine. Pendant ce repas, nous avons vu aux informations télévisées notre Président Emanuel MACRON en visite en Chine.

Mon grand-père connait bien la Chine, il m'a expliqué que notre président a choisi Xi'an comme la 1ère ville de sa visite, Xi'an était le point de départ et retour de l'ancienne route de la soie. Si notre président a choisi Xi'an, il y a surement un lien avec la nouvelle route de la soie.

Je ne comprenais pas la nouvelle route de la soie. Mon papi m'a dit qu'il y a très longtemps, des commerçants chinois intelligents sont partis de la ville de Xi'an et ont transporté des marchandises en Europe, c'était la route de la soie par voie de terre. Ensuite il y avait la route de la soie maritime qui transportait les marchandises par bateau entre la Chine et les reste du monde.

Aujourd'hui cette nouvelle route de la soie est comme un pont qui relie la Chine au reste du monde. Beaucoup de trains sont chargés des marchandises partent des villes chinoises vers l'Europe, par exemple, il y a un train de marchandise direct de Chengdu à Lodz, également de Wuhan à Lyon. Papi a dit que désormais les sacs à dos qu'il va acheter en Chine pourront prendre le train pour arriver à Lyon, il est rapide et pratique.

Je trouve cela super, et j'ai dit que, désormais, si j'envoie des cadeaux à mes amis en Chine, les cadeaux vont voyager dans le train pendant une dizaine de jours avant d'arriver chez mes amis. De plus, il sera très facile pour moi de voir mes amis chinois.

Avec mes parents, nous vous remercions de nous donner la chance de fêter le nouvel an chinois à Chengdu, de découvrir la culture chinoise. Je suis très content et j'ai partagé cette bonne nouvelle avec ma maitresse. Ma maitresse m'a dit de bien profiter du voyage et de partager mon expérience avec mes copains dès mon retour en France.

Yanis

我眼中的"一带一路"

龙阳（法国）

大家好，我叫 Yanis Laine，我的中文名字叫龙阳，我很快就满8岁了，我住在法国里昂旁边的一个小城市。我上小学二年级，平时最喜欢踢足球，也喜欢玩电子游戏。

2018年1月7日是一个周日，我的爸爸、妈妈带着我和小妹妹去爷爷家庆祝主显节，一起品尝传统的国王饼。爷爷家的厨房装有电视，所以我们一边吃饭，一边看电视，从新闻里得知我们的总统马克龙就在当天要出发去访问中国。

我爷爷非常了解中国，他说马克龙总统去中国的第一站西安就是古丝绸之路的起点和终点。而这次马克龙去访问中国首选西安，看来与"一带一路"有关系。

我不明白什么是"一带一路"，爷爷告诉我，在很久以前，有很多聪明的中国商人从西安出发，将中国的东西运到

▲法国小记者龙阳及家人在金沙遗址博物馆

了欧洲，这就是过去的陆上丝绸之路，后来又有了海上丝绸之路，通过各种大船把货物从中国发往世界各地。

现在的"一带一路"就像一座大桥，把中国和世界各地紧紧地连接在一起，有很多大火车装满了货物，络绎不绝地从中国的城市开往欧洲，比如成都有直接开往波兰罗兹的货物列车，武汉也有直接开往法国里昂的货物列车。爷爷说以后他在中国供货商那里购买的背包就可以通过火车运到里昂了，既方便又节省时间。

▲法国小记者龙阳在永陵向成都的爷爷学舞剑

我听了后觉得太棒了，我说以后如果我要寄礼物给我的中国小朋友，那就让礼物在火车上玩十几天就到朋友的家了，而且要见中国的朋友也会很容易了。

非常感谢成都市广播电视台的叔叔阿姨给我这么一个好机会，让我和父母能够亲自去成都欢度中国的春节，了解中国的文化。我高兴得乐呵呵的，还把这个好消息告诉了我的老师，我的老师鼓励我好好体验领会"中国行的意义和乐趣"，回到法国后和同学们分享这段千载难逢的经历。

来自加拿大的

卡桑德拉·阿尔梅达 & 马库斯

Why I Want to Go to China

Cassandra Almeida (Canada)

My name is Cassandra Almeida. I can't believe I'm actually going to China with my brother Marcus and my mom Chantal! But my dad is staying home because he has to work. I have a lot of reasons why I really want to go to China, here are a few. One of my reasons is that I love pandas. They're cute and snug and curious. Also, I can't wait to go to the panda sanctuary. I want to see the pandas. My goal is to pet a panda yet the panda sanctuary is probably not a petting zoo. There are 1,864 giant pandas in the wild in China. I also saw a really cute video of pandas hugging. How adorable!

I want to tell you a story about my best friend. Her name is Lindsay. Her mom Lulu is Chinese. Lindsay is Chinese too. She was born in China. One time Lindsay's family invited our family to come have dinner with them. I tried Chinese food and it was really yummy. We had these chicken wings and rice and other foods that I really liked. I hope we have this Chinese food every night when we are in China. I'm really excited to try all the other foods in China. I'm really excited for Chinese New Year. I would like to try to play the Chinese games and eat chocolate honey and see the Dragon. I have read about Chinese New Year in books and I feel it is very fun, so I'm excited to go. I'm excited to see the fireworks. When I was little I was afraid of fireworks because they were way too loud for me. I was also reminded about the zodiac wheel and I was born in the year of the rat. I wonder what special things they do for the year of the dog.

I've never been to China before. My friend Lindsay has been to China many times because a lot of her family live in China. I've been to Cuba and Nova Scotia, which is a province of Canada. Canada is such a big country that I feel like other places in Canada are a different country. I would also like to see other countries. I can't wait to go to the city of Chengdu. I live in Aurora, Ontario. The city of Aurora has about 53,000 people. I just found out the city of Chengdu has 14,430,000 people! That is a really cool fact! I'm excited and very nervous. I really hope there's a translator to help me talk to the Chinese people. I can't wait until I'm on the plane and going on all these really awesome adventures.

We're going to take two airplane trips, we're going to stop at South Korea and then we're going to go to China. I'm very excited to be in South Korea for about 5 hours. I would love to see the Great Wall of China, but I'm not sure that I'll get to because I don't know if we're going to be close to the Great Wall of China. I'm also very excited to see the panda sanctuary. I wonder what the house staying in looks like. I'm also going to the Chengdu Temple Fair. I can't wait to see all the beautiful lights and try the sugar animals that I found out about. I don't know what other adventures I'm going to go on, but I do hope that we go on a lot more adventures while I am in China.

I'm very excited to go to China! I think it'll be a really fun experience and I can't wait to go on TV and all the other fun things that I'm going to do on the trip. I'm so so happy to get this opportunity for myself and my family.

为什么我想去中国

卡桑德拉·阿尔梅达（加拿大）

　　我叫卡桑德拉·阿尔梅达。真不敢相信，我竟然要和妈妈尚塔尔及兄弟马库斯一起去中国！可爸爸得待在家里，因为工作离不开。我有很多想去中国的理由，其中之一是我喜欢熊猫。它们憨态可掬，讨人喜欢。我很期待去保护区看熊猫。我的理想是养只宠物熊猫，但熊猫保护区可不是宠物动物园。在中国，有1864只大熊猫生活在野外。我看过一个非常可爱的"熊猫抱"视频。真的太可爱了！

　　我想告诉你一个关于我最好的朋友的故事，她的名字叫林赛。她妈妈露露是中国人。林赛是中国人，出生在中国。记得林赛的家人曾邀请我们全家一起共进晚餐。中国菜味道很好。我们吃了鸡翅、米饭和其他一些食物，我都喜欢。希望我们去中国的时候，也能吃到当晚那样美味的东西。我真的很期待能尝尝其他的中国菜，也同样期待中国的新年。我想玩中国游戏，吃巧克力糖，看舞龙。我读过有关中国新年的书，觉得很有趣，所以很想去。我很盼望去看烟花。小时候，我害怕放爆竹，那声音太响了。我记得中国有**十二属相**的说法，而我是属鼠的。我很好奇人们在狗年做什么特别的

小贴士

十二属相：中国古代数术家拿十二种地支配十二种动物（子、丑、寅、卯、辰、巳、午、未、申、酉、戌、亥、配鼠、牛、虎、兔、龙、蛇、马、羊、猴、鸡、狗、猪）即十二生肖（属相）。见《论衡·物势》，后以人生在某年即肖（xiào）某物。外国亦有这种纪年方法，在印度为鼠、牛、狮子、兔等，在希腊为牡牛、山羊、狮子等。

事情。

我以前从未去过中国。我的朋友林赛已经去过中国很多次了，因为她的许多亲人都住在中国。我去过古巴和加拿大的新斯科舍省。加拿大

是一个很大的国家，我觉得安大略省以外的地方简直就是外国。我想看看其他国家是啥样。我迫不及待地想去成都。我家住在安大略省奥罗拉市。奥罗拉市大约有5.3万人。我刚发现成都人口多达1443万！真是太酷了！我又兴奋又紧张，我真的希望有个翻译能帮助我与中国人交谈。我巴不得立刻上飞机，开启真正的冒险之旅。

我们的飞行路程分为两段，先在韩国转机，然后再飞中国。我很乐意在韩国待上5个小时。我很想去看看中国的长城，但不知道行不行，因为不清楚我们将要去的地方是否靠近长城。我也很高兴能去熊猫保护区。不知道熊猫的家是什么样的。我还要去成都庙会。我迫不及待地想欣赏美丽的灯会，品尝糖人儿。不知道在中国还有什么别的活动，但愿我们能经历更多的冒险。

我很高兴能去中国！这肯定会是一次非常有趣的体验，我迫不及待地想上电视，想参与旅途中其他有趣的活动。我很高兴能为我和家人赢得这次机会。

Appendix: The Travel Feelings of Marcus and Cassandra

Marcus（Cassandra's Brother）

I liked the market where I got a goldfish! I loved my backpack and I was very happy I got a certificate like my sister. I liked the dancers on stage. I fell asleep on the hot pot table because I was still very tired travelling from Canada. I liked everything!

Cassandra

My favourite part of the past two days was the 4D movie. At the temple I learned that people built that thousands of years ago, it was interesting. I could't believe how big it is inside and it was like a cave. I liked to try the swords with the lady outside.

The first day at the dinner, I saw the mask at the restaurant on the ground in the tile after we learned about it at the museum. I was excited to recognize it. I liked the dancers at the restaurant and the fire out of the puppets' mouths. The hot pot was fun and my favourite food was the eggs. The craft ink was a bit difficult to use, but it turned out good in the end.

I am very happy and thankful that I got this opportunity.

附：马库斯与卡桑德拉成都之行的感悟

马库斯（卡桑德拉的弟弟）

我喜欢逛自由市场，在这里我买了一条金鱼！我很喜欢背包，也很高兴像姐姐一样拿到了证书。我喜欢舞台上的舞蹈演员。吃火锅的当儿我睡着了，因为从加拿大到这里的长途旅行太累了。总之，我喜欢这儿的一切！

卡桑德拉

在过去的两天里，我最喜欢的是4D电影。另外，我得知我们参观的寺庙是在几千年前建造的，这很有趣。我简直不敢相信里面有多大，就像一个深深的洞穴。我真想和外面的女士一起比画刀剑。

第一天，我们在参观博物馆时看到一个面具，之后，在餐厅的地砖上我又看到了。我很高兴自己认出来了。我也喜欢餐厅里的舞蹈和木偶吐火的节目。火锅很好吃，我最喜欢吃的是鸡蛋。学习书法时研墨有点难，不过后来还算顺利。

我很高兴有这个机会，非常感谢大家。

来自越南的阮光明

Quang Minh - Việt Nam

Em rất vui vì đây là lần đầu tiên em được đặt chân ra nước ngoài. Trung Quốc nổi bật với con người, cũng như nền văn hóa, nền kinh tế và đa dạng hệ sinh thái. Lịch sử của Trung Quốc cũng đã góp phần không ít để dựng lên những kỳ quan của nơi này. Còn về phong cảnh thì phải nói là rất đẹp: những hàng cây xanh mướt, những bồn hoa thơm, và cả một "mê cung" đầy những tòa nhà cao tầng và xe cộ ở trong thành phố. Nhưng em thích nhất vẫn là truyền thống đặc sắc và phong tục cổ xưa của người Trung Quốc, chẳng hạn như: múa kiếm, lễ hội, hội chợ Tết... Em hi vọng sau chuyến đi này sẽ học được những điều hay và kì thú từ đất nước Trung Quốc.

A Brilliant Journey to China

Quang Micnh（Viet Nam）

I am very happy because this is the first time I go abroad. China is known for its people as well as culture, economy and a diverse eco-system. The country's history has also helped establish beauty spots here. The scenery is also very beautiful with lines of green trees, fragrant flowers and a lot of tall buildings and vehicles in the city. But what I like most are Chinese traditional customs, which are very original and colourful, such as sword performance, festivals, New Year fairs, etc. I hope that after the visit I can learn many interesting things from China.

光明的中国之旅

阮光明（越南）

这是我第一次出国，我感到非常高兴。中国以发达的经济、文化，众多的人口及多元的生态系统而闻名于世。中国历史悠久，景色优美，处处绿水青山花红柳绿，名胜古迹相互掩映，城市里有很多高高的建筑，车流人潮井然有序。而我最爱的是中国传统习俗，丰富多彩，富有创意，比如舞剑、春节的各种庆祝仪式等。我希望此次旅程能让我了解更多有关中国的趣事。

来自俄罗斯的
瓦西里萨

A Special Trip to China

Vasilisa (Russia)

Hello! My name is Vasilisa. I live in Moscow, Russia. I'm 10 years old. I'm a student of Grade 5. My family is big. There are 6 members: mother, father, 2 older sisters and a younger sister. I have a dog. I love rhythmic gymnastic and I'm practicing it 5 days a week. I want to be a champion.

In Russia we meet Chinese people and Chinese culture in movies and everyday life. We have noodle maker machine at home. I love to cook noodle together with my sisters. I know noodle is very popular in China as well. Everybody knows the movie *Kung-fu Panda*. The panda is one of my favorite characters. We have many goods made in China like smartphones, computers, clothing, home supplies, etc. In Moscow we have Chinese food restaurants. I love to drink tea and I know that tea came to our country from China. I never thought how these goods made in China are delivered to our country.

When I came to Chengdu, besides many interesting things, I met very friendly and enthusiastic people. Everybody was smiling and happy to see us. I visited Chengdu International Railway Harbor and I could see now it is working very well and makes connection between our countries much easier. I liked sites we had seen. And I was amazed of the show in local community, especially by acrobatic wushu and dance of face changing. I liked Chinese food which was delicious, and I liked sweets very much. I was impressed that in the apartment of our host family there was an exit on the roof. And there was a small garden on the roof. I was amazed that in Chengdu there is no snow in winter but flowers and green trees are everywhere.

特别的中国之行

瓦西里萨（俄罗斯）

　　大家好。我的名字叫瓦西里萨，住在俄罗斯莫斯科，今年10岁，是一名五年级的学生。我有个大家庭，父母亲和2个姐姐、1个妹妹，共6个成员。还有一只狗。我爱跳韵律操，每周练习5天。我想成为一名冠军。

　　在俄罗斯日常生活和电影中，常常会遇到中国人和中国文化。我知道面条在中国很受欢迎。我家有制面机。我喜欢和我的姐妹们一起做面

▲给俄罗斯小记者接机

▲俄罗斯小记者瓦西里萨在启动仪式现场

条。在俄罗斯，大家对电影《功夫熊猫》耳熟能详。《功夫熊猫》是我最喜欢的影片之一。俄罗斯有很多中国商品，比如智能手机、电脑、服装、家居用品等。在莫斯科还有中餐馆。我喜欢品茶，我知道茶是从中国传来的。我从未想过这些中国商品是如何运送到我们国家的。

来成都的时候，我碰到许多有趣的事情，这里的人们也很友好热情。每个人都面带微笑，很高兴见到我们。我参观了成都国际铁路港，可以看到它现在运作得很好，便利了我们两国之间的交通。我喜欢我们参观的地方。让我印象深刻的是当地社区的演出，尤其是技艺惊人的武术和瞬息万变的变脸。中国菜很好吃，我很喜欢，尤其喜欢吃甜食。我印象深刻的是，在我们寄宿家庭的公寓里，屋顶上有一个出口，通往一个小花园。成都冬天不下雪，处处鲜花绿树，这让我很惊讶。

来自德国的
雅各布

Der Zug zwischen China und Europa, eine coole Verbindung

Tu Jakob Tiancheng

Fast jeder kleine Junge ist von der Eisenbahn fasziniert. Ich bin da keine Ausnahme. Ich, in Europa aufwachsen, bekam schon sehr früh in den Armen meiner Mutter oder meines Vaters die Geschichten von Thomas, der kleinen Lokomotive, vorgelesen. Später bekam ich eine Holzeisenbahn geschenkt und verlegte ihre Schienen durch die ganze Wohnung. Meine Mutter sagt, dass eines der ersten Wörter, die ich gesprochen habe, „Eisenbahn" gewesen ist. Meine Mutter und mein Vater erkannten früh mein Interesse an der Eisenbahn und nahmen mich zu einem echten Bahnhof mit. Das war ein sehr aufregender Moment! Dort gab es lange Züge, die aus von mir unbekannten Orten kamen und mit lautem Getöse wieder in der Ferne verschwanden. Und dann sind wir sogar in einen dieser Wagen mit vielen Sitzen gestiegen und damit zu einer mir bis dahin unbekannten Stadt gefahren, wo wir entfernte Verwandte besuchten.

Meine deutschen Großeltern leben in einiger Entfernung von uns, und wenn wir sie besuchen entscheiden wir uns meistens für den Zug. Im Auto im Kindersitz angeschnallt zu sein hat mir nie gefallen. Zwar hat mein Vater immer wieder mal Pausen gemacht, aber dadurch kamen wir immer sehr spät bei meinen Großeltern an. Wenn mir jedoch in der Eisenbahn langweilig wurde konnte ich mit meinem Vater durch den ganzen Zug laufen. Wenn der Schaffner kam bekam ich immer eine bunte Kinderfahrkarte geschenkt. Inzwischen sind viele Jahre vergangen und ich bin nicht mehr zappelig.

Mama hat sich immer neue Spiele ausgedacht und einmal kam ihr eine Idee, als wir im Bahnhof der kleinen Stadt, in der meine Großeltern leben, auf den Zug warten mussten. Ein Zug fuhr durch und plötzlich rief Mama: „Schau mal, die kommen aus China!" Ich sah einen Güterzug mit lauter großen Kisten. Meine Eltern erklärten mir, dass darin viele verschiedene Dinge sind, zum Beispiel Lebensmittel, Spielsachen und Kleidung. Sie sagten, dass man diese Kisten Container nennt.

Mama zeigte mir die Container, die aus China kamen. Weil sie mit chinesischen Schriftzeichen bemalt waren, waren sie von den anderen Containern gut zu unterscheiden. Mama entdeckte in dem schnell durchfahrenden Zug drei Container aus China. Von da an hatten wir ein neues Spiel. Wenn wir auf unseren Zug zurück nach Berlin warten mussten und ein Güterzug durchfuhr zählten wir die Container aus China. Meine Großeltern wohnen in einer kleinen Stadt nicht weit weg von Hamburg und Duisburg. Daher ist es kein Wunder, dass dort häufig Güterzüge vorbei fahren. Jedenfalls sehen wir sie dort oft.

Weil ich die Eisenbahn so sehr mag sind Mama und Papa mit mir sehr oft mit Zügen gefahren, in Deutschland, Frankreich, Polen und China. In Schnellzügen, Nahverkehrszügen, Oldtimerzüge, Doppelstockwagen, eine alte Schmalspurbahn in Jiayang bei Zigong in Sichuan und ein Nachtzug von Chengdu nach Xi'an. In Chinas Hochgeschwindigkeitszügen bin ich auch schon gefahren. Sie sind bequem und schnell. Mit meinen Eltern gehe ich auch oft ins Eisenbahnmuseum. Deswegen weiß ich immer mehr über die Geschichte und die technische Entwicklung der Eisenbahn.

Ich erinnere mich noch, wie wir einmal nach Weihnachten wieder auf dem kleinen Bahnhof meiner Großeltern auf unseren Zug nach Berlin warteten. Dort ist es sehr ruhig und es gibt nur wenige Reisende. Nicht so wie auf den Berliner Bahnhöfen, wo es immer laut ist und viele Menschen sind. Hier ist man den Zügen viel näher und mit den schönen Villen, den Dörfern und der Natur im Hintergrund habe ich das Gefühl mich wieder in einer Geschichte von Thomas, der kleinen Lokomotive, zu befinden. In den letzten Jahren haben wir immer häufiger Güterzüge mit chinesischen Containern vorbeifahren sehen. Wir drei in unserer Familie haben sie immer gezählt, aber meistens hatte jeder ein anderes Ergebnis, weil es so viele waren. Diesmal sagte Mama plötzlich zu mir: „Jakob, es gibt nun einen Güterzug, der direkt von China nach Duisburg fährt. Da müssen wir die Container nicht zu zählen, denn sie kommen alle aus China. Dieser Zug nimmt den gleichen Weg wie die Seidenstraße, von der du schon mal gehört hast. Diese Zugverbindung ist Teil eines Projektes, welches man „One Belt, One Road" oder auch „Neue Seidenstraße" nennt. Dieser Zug legt von Osten nach Westen dreizehntausend Kilometer zurück und verbindet mehr als 50 Länder und Regionen. Es ist die längste Zugstrecke der Welt. Pro Woche pendeln 25 Züge zwischen China und Deutschland. Ihr Endziel in Deutschland ist Duisburg, was ganz in der Nähe der Geburtsstadt deiner Oma, nämlich Düsseldorf, liegt."

Wow, das war das erste Mal, dass ich von diesem Zug hörte. Echt cool! Aus Spaß habe ich meine Mutter gefragt, ob sie mich in eine Sache verwandeln kann, die dann mit dem Güterzug bis nach Chengdu gebracht wird, damit ich meine chinesischen Großeltern, die dort leben, besuchen kann. In Chengdu gibt es auch viele Kinder, mit denen ich das Brettspiel Go spielen kann.

Mama weiß, dass Go spielen seit zwei Jahren eines meiner Lieblingshobbys ist. Sie hat gelacht und gesagt: „Nun, du weißt vom Go-Spiel, dass nur die Steine, die miteinander verbunden sind, stärker sind und überleben können. So ist das auch mit der Zugverbindung zwischen China und Europa. Durch den Austausch von Waren wird die Wirtschaft aller Länder gestärkt, die von dem Projekt betroffen sind.

Du spielst sowohl in Deutschland als auch in China mit deinen kleinen und großen Freunden Go. Du weißt, dass man das auch „Handtalk" nennt. Go ist eine Quintessenz der chinesischen Kultur und Philosophie. Wenn du Go spielst ist das also wie ein Kulturaustausch. Nur wenn sich Länder untereinander kulturell austauschen können sie sich besser verstehen.

Ich bin erst 12 Jahre alt. Ich muss noch ein paar Jahre warten, bevor ich eine ähnliche Aufgabe übernehmen kann wie der Zug zwischen China und Europa. Aber mit den kleinen schwarzen und weißen Go-Steinen in der Hand verbinde ich die Chinesen und Europäer, die ich kenne. Das ist eine gute Idee. Eigentlich habe ich mit diesem „Zug" schon angefangen.

中欧班列，好酷的连接

雅各布（德国）

几乎每个男孩小时候都痴迷于火车，我也不例外。在欧洲长大的我们，小时候都在爸爸妈妈怀里听过托马斯小火车的故事，然后很快就会得到一套带轨道的玩具火车，而家里的过道就成了铁路沿线。妈妈说，在我刚学会的那几个单词里，说得最多的就是"火车"。我的爸爸妈妈善于发现我的兴趣所在，很快，他们就带我去了真正的火车站。那是一个令人兴奋的时刻！长长的火车从神秘

的远方开来，威风凛凛地从眼前呼啸而过，很快又消失在轨道尽头。我们不只是看看，爸爸妈妈紧接着带我进入这个有着长长空间和许多座椅的长龙里，让它把我们全家带到一个新的地方，在那里会见到几个平时不常见的亲爱的家人。

我的爷爷奶奶住的地方与我们有一段距离，去看他们时，爸爸妈妈常常选择坐火车。虽然爸爸可以开车去，但我长时间被绑在汽车儿童座

椅上并不是件舒服的事，当然爸爸也可经常停车，但老停的话，到奶奶家就很晚了。在火车上，我要是坐烦了的话，爸爸总会陪我穿过长长的过道从车头走到车尾，碰到列车员还可向他要张儿童卡通车票。多少年来，就这样来来去去，我慢慢长大了，也没有那么坐不住了。

每次坐火车时，妈妈总会发明一些新的游戏。有一次，在我们等车的小站台边，她又想出了一个新点子。当时，一列火车正从我们眼前疾驰而过，她像突然发现了什么似的兴奋地对我喊："快看，乖乖，中国来的！中国来的！中国来的！"我顺着她的手指看过去，已认出这是一列货运火车，载

▲德国小记者在启动仪式上分享活动感受

的都是大箱子。听说箱子里面是各种各样的东西，吃的、玩的、穿的，什么都有。后来，我知道这叫集装箱。她要我看的原来是中国来的集装箱，箱体上与众不同的方块字很显眼，与其他尽是拼音字母的大箱子很容易区别开来。她对着飞奔的列车重复说了三次"中国来的"，大概是她看到了三个来自中国的集装箱吧。从那时开始，我们每次在这个小火车站等候去柏林的火车时，就多了一个全家人玩的游戏，那就是数数有多少中国来的集装箱！奶奶住的这个小城在德国中西部，离汉堡海港和内陆港杜伊斯堡都不远，难怪总有货运火车从这里经过，所以我们会常常碰到！

出于对火车的热爱，爸爸妈妈带我坐了各种各样的火车。德国的、法国的、波兰的、中国的……这些火车，有快车、慢车，有像二战电影中的东欧火车，有透过车窗可以看到更远风景的双层列车，还有中国四川乐山市犍为嘉阳煤矿的运煤小火车，特别是成都到西安的卧铺夜车，可以在上面美美睡一觉，这在面积不大的德国可是不容易体验到的。中国的高铁，真是又宽敞又舒适。我还经常跟爸爸妈妈去火车博物馆，了解火车的历史变迁、技术发展等，有关火车的知识我知道得越来越多了。

记得有年圣诞节后，拜望完爷爷奶奶的我们又站在了那个小火车站台上。比起柏林大火车站的嘈杂、人流的挤迫，这里很清净，等车的人并不多，在这里看过往的火车时是那么逼近，旁边的别墅、村落、自然风光的衬托仿佛让我们又跳进了托马斯故事的画面里。我们一家三口比着数来数去，最后数字总有出入。这一次，妈妈突然说："雅各布，有一趟不用数，它是从中国直接开到

德国杜伊斯堡的中欧班列，全是中国的集装箱！这趟火车走的是你所知道的丝绸之路一样的路线，是一个现在被叫作'一带一路'的新丝绸之路的很重要的一个组成部分。还有，这列火车运输距离东西长1.3万余公

里，连通了50多个国家和地区，是世界上行程最长的火车！到德国的这列火车每周多达25趟，在德国停靠的是奶奶的家乡杜塞尔多夫旁边的杜伊斯堡！"

哇，第一次听说有这样的一列火车。真酷！我开玩笑地跟妈妈说，你可不可以把我变成货物装进这趟列车去体会体会，直接从德国坐到中国成都去看望外公外婆！还可以找成都的小朋友下围棋呢！

妈妈知道我这两年来的几个爱好之一是下围棋。她笑着说："好啊！你看你下围棋时，对棋子来说，连接在一起才可以强大、才有生命力。我们中国人现在驶出这趟列车，连接沿路的许多国家和地区一同来发展经济，让欧洲人用上了许多中国商品。你在德国、中国都在跟大小朋友们下围棋，'手谈'。围棋里就有中国传统文化中哲学思想的精髓，这是一种文化的连接。大家多交流才会相互理解！"

我才12岁，也许过几年才能参与中欧班列承载的任务。不过，用我手上小小的黑白棋子，连接上我所认识的中国人、德国人，其他欧洲人，这个主意也不错。事实上，我们已经开始这样做了。

"熊猫·小·记者" 行动 的 报道

8月以来，"熊猫小记者"全球追访"一带一路"大型公益新闻接力行动在全球多个国家进行。40余名中国"熊猫小记者"分为张骞队、郑和队、马可·波罗队，前往欧亚多国开展"一带一路"沿线国家的交流活动。8月1日，熊猫小记者们拜访了中国驻波兰大使馆，采访了大使和使馆官员；2号又前往蓉欧快铁终点站罗兹，了解更多关于"一带一路"的精彩中国故事。

——摘自央视新闻频道《新闻直播间》2018年8月10日关于"熊猫小记者"的报道

"熊猫小记者"全球追访"一带一路"大型公益新闻接力行动今年再次被国家广电总局列为2018年度"丝绸之路影视桥工程"重点项目之一。同去年相比，今年的活动在线路规划上，更加注重体验"一带一路"建设的重大成果和与当地中小学生的互动交流，更加注重活动的国际影响力和传播力。

——摘自《中国新闻》2018年7月30关于"熊猫小记者"的报道

2017年8月9日电　当地时间9日，13名"熊猫小记者"全球追访"一带一路"大型公益新闻接力行动"马可·波罗队"的小记者们从法国斯特拉斯堡抵达南部重要港口城市马赛，以他们独特的视角在当地展开"一带一路"下"中国印迹"的探寻。

这群"熊猫小记者"年龄从8岁到14岁不等，穿梭在马赛市中心最大的家乐福超市，通过寻找货架上的"中国货"，了解中国产品的销售情况，切身感受中国制造给当地民众生活带来的影响，体验互联互通给贸易往来、互通有无带来的便利。

——摘自人民网2017年8月9日关于"熊猫小记者"行动的报道

人民网8月7日电　"'熊猫小记者'全球追访'一带一路'大型公益新闻接力行动"马可·波罗队的12名小成员当地时间8月6日走进中国驻荷兰大使馆，与使馆领导及工作人员畅谈欧洲之行的收获和感悟，为追访之旅画上了圆满的句号。

"熊猫小记者"马可·波罗队此行从德国的慕尼黑出发，在十天的行程中走访了德国、比利时、荷兰的多座重要城市，用少年人的独特视角深入观察着"一带一路"沿线国家的风土人情、文化魅力，用亲身经历感受着中欧间交流沟通的迷人画面、感人故事。

——摘自人民网2018年8月7日关于"熊猫小记者"行动的报道

近日，全球追访"一带一路"大型公益新闻接力行动的"熊猫小记者"们抵达捷克。8月9日，十余名"熊猫小记者"参观了中国驻捷克大使馆，并和使馆工作人员进行交流。小记者们首先参观了使馆对外大厅，观看了"丝路新颜"和"八一建军节"主题图片展，了解使馆工作情况。随后，他们与使馆文化参赞吴光交流互动，纷纷举手提问，现场气氛热烈。吴光参赞高度评价小记者们对捷克和"一带一路"建设的关注，回答了小记者们关于中捷文化交流的有关问题。她希望小记者们能够充分利用这次机会认识捷克、了解捷克，不但要向捷克民众展示中国小学生积极向上的精神面貌，还要把在捷克的所见所感带回中国，促进两国青少年之间的相互了解。

——摘自中华人民共和国驻捷克共和国大使馆官方网站2017年8月14日关于"熊猫小记者"行动的报道

新华社罗马8月14日电　来自四川成都的13名马可·波罗队"熊猫小记者"继访问意大利威尼斯之后，13日又走进罗马的中国驻意大利大使馆，并采访了使馆新闻处主任张爱山。刚一见面，"熊猫小记者"彭铃欢就将代表成都的卡通熊猫送给了张爱山。小记者们讲述了他们在欧洲的见闻和思考，包括他们眼中的意大利文化、成都与意大利的经贸往来、意大利人对中国"一带一路"建设的看法、"一带一路"建设对意大利的影响等，并准备了一堆问题向外交官发问。马可·波罗队本月11日抵达威尼斯，通过在圣马可广场上的"快闪"等活动，向当地居民和来自世界各地的游客介绍中国以及大熊猫的故乡成都。无论是演唱歌曲《茉莉花》，还是朗诵古诗《春夜喜雨》，小记者们的出现总会引起游人的注意，也受到媒体关注。

——摘自新华社2017年8月14日关于"熊猫小记者"行动的报道

2018年8月1日，驻波兰大使刘光源会见成都市广播电视台组派的"熊猫小记者"张骞队一行16人并接受"熊猫小记者"采访，文化参赞蔡炼等人参加会见。刘大使向大家简述了中波两国传统友好历史，并介绍了两国在"一带一路"和"16+1合作"框架下积极开展各领域交流合作现状，特别是习近平主席2016年成功访问波兰、建立全面战略伙伴关系将两国友好合作推到新高度，并就"熊猫小记者"所提出的大使的工作是什么、使馆如何开展外交工作、从成都出发到波兰罗兹的中欧班列货运等问题——作答。刘大使希望"熊猫小记者"们通过这次中东欧之行，多看、多学、多思，携手当地小朋友关心和支持"一带一路"建设，努力成为中波两国人民友谊的传播者和践行者。

——摘自中华人民共和国驻波兰共和国大使馆官方网站2018年8月1日关于"熊猫小记者"行动的报道

8月11日，参加全球追访"一带一路"大型公益新闻接力活动的"熊猫小记者"(马可·波罗队)抵达马可·波罗故乡水城威尼斯。十余名"熊猫小记者"在威尼斯最负盛名的圣马可广场向游人们介绍"一带一路"，介绍中国，介绍成都。小记者们说，"一带一路"倡议对沿线国家经贸交往的重要性不言而喻，虽然他们年龄还小，但仍然可以在加强与各国青少年的文化交流方面作出贡献。

——摘自光明网及《光明日报》2017年8月14日关于"熊猫小记者"行动的报道

在青白江区成都国际铁路港现代物流大厦发布厅内，40名小朋友身着白色T恤、手持五彩队旗，参加在这里举行的"'熊猫小记者'全球追访'一带一路'大型公益新闻接力行动（第二季）"出发仪式。从今天起，40名小朋友将兵分三路，分别前往欧洲、亚洲的9个"一带一路"沿线国家，用小记者的视角记录沿线国家人文景致，在探寻"一带一路"战略的深刻内涵的同时，传递文化、交流情感。此次全球追访行动，三支队伍在对外交流、采访报道的同时，还将向"一带一路"沿线国家的小朋友和家庭发出邀请，成为推广天府文化、传递古蜀文明的使者。此外，"熊猫小记者"们通过沿途走访抒写的文章还将汇编成书籍，面向全国公开发行。

——摘自《成都商报》2018年7月29日关于"熊猫小记者"行动的报道

新华社波兰罗兹8月2日电 "中欧班列（蓉欧快铁）让成都与罗兹的关系更紧密了，具体表现在哪些方面？"带着这个问题，"'熊猫小记者'全球追访'一带一路'大型公益新闻接力行动"张骞队的10名小记者2日探访"一带一路"重要节点城市波兰罗兹市。罗兹市政府负责国际合作与投资的办公室副主任莫妮卡·卡罗尔查克热情接待了他们。

卡罗尔查克回答说，罗兹至成都的中欧班列已经运营5年，近年来两市保持密切合作交流，结为国际友好城市。波兰在成都设立总领事馆，成都与波兰的经贸多元化合作、教育和民间交往更加便利。

孩子们在采访的同时，也被特地赶来的当地TOYA网络电视台记者当成采访对象。"你们喜欢波兰吗，对什么印象深刻？""你可以介绍'熊猫小记者'项目吗？""你们还去了哪些国家？"一连串问题抛了过来。

来自四川甘孜藏族自治州的吴珂优有条不紊地答道："'熊猫小记者'项目是通过走访'一带一路'沿线国家，使我们更加深入地了解这些国家的文化。波兰是第一站。接下来，我们还将去捷克和匈牙利。"

——摘自新华社、新华网2018年8月2日关于"熊猫小记者"行动的报道

国际在线报道：2018年7月31日，"熊猫小记者"全球追访"一带一路"大型公益新闻接力行动第二季在德国慕尼黑正式启动。"熊猫小记者"马可·波罗队将以德国慕尼黑为起点，用自己独特的视角深入探访"一带一路"沿线国家的历史风貌和当代发展状况，深刻体会中外文化的交流与融合，努力成长为连接中国与世界的文明使者。

——摘凤凰网、国际在线2018年7月31日关于"熊猫小记者"行动的报道

成都的郫县豆瓣、简阳的火锅底料、眉山的榨菜、德阳的青稞麦饼……小记者们进入超市后，很快找到了来自中国的各类食品，其中包括不少成都及四川各地的商品。小记者夏文涛说："看到成都的美食传播到这里，特别是看到了我们简阳的火锅底料，我感到太惊讶了。"小记者陈彦旭也表示没想到这里有那么多"中国制造"："我觉得很自豪。"在万里之外的比利时找到了家乡的食品、找到来自中国的货物，也让小记者们真切地感受到，"一带一路"倡议不仅让更多的中国产品走出国门，让更多的四川食品进入比利时的家庭，而且通过饮食文化交流，也会拉近成都乃至四川与世界的距离。他们相信，未来将会有更多更好的中国产品通过"一带一路"走向世界。

——摘自国际在线2018年8月5日关于"熊猫小记者"行动的报道